CW00536148

Praise for this book

"This is amazing – a tribute to not just your experience but your ability to track all the crazy mishaps! I would imagine new and seasoned presenters would love to have this! It's worth an arm and a leg to avoid all the pitfalls we have all had!"

Anne Bishop, Insights Learning and Development Canada

"I started it yesterday and all I can say is it's F'ING fantastic! I started at the beginning in-between doing other things and I was completely drawn in. I can certainly learn a lot from it. I like the practicality (slides as landing deck pre session) - the examples (especially the ARM and LEG metaphor) - the down to earth nature of it. You are an excellent writer, and you say things clearly and effectively. I love how you tied in famous people to the examples of going the extra mile too (James Brown…trimming the fat - pro athletes!)"

Kim White, Pacific Collaborative Inc.

About this book

The Covid-19 pandemic has forced us all to become web presenters or participants – or both. Whether you're attending Teams meetings with co-workers, the monthly Zoom meeting of your garden club, or presenting online learning to others, the need to understand and properly use webinar software is now more important than ever.

We also know many companies will continue to incorporate virtual learning into their employee training programs long after Covid-19 becomes endemic. This means adopting best practices and becoming more professional in the way we host or show up in these virtual connections.

This book delivers the details on how to design and facilitate learning in the virtual space. Whether you're a presenter or a participant, this book outlines the building blocks of creating an educational, informative, and engaging webinar.

Copyright ©2021 by Dale Nelson. All rights reserved.

Published by BookBaby
7905 N. Crescent Blvd., Pennsauken, NJ 08110

All rights reserved. No part of this publication may be reproduced, distributed, or transmitted in any form or by any means, including photocopying, recording, or other electronic or mechanical methods, without the prior written permission of the publisher, except in the case of brief quotations embodied in critical reviews and certain other non-commercial uses permitted by copyright law. For permission requests, contact the author at dale@professionalwebinars.com

Limit of Liability/Disclaimer of Warranty:
While the publisher and author have used their best effort in preparing this book, they make no representations or warranties with respect to the accuracy or completeness of the contents of this book and specifically disclaim any implied warranties of merchantability or fitness for a particular purpose. No warranty may be created or extended by sales representatives or written sales materials. The advice and strategies contained herein may not be suitable for your situation. You should consult with a professional where appropriate. Neither the publisher nor author shall be liable for any loss of profit or any other commercial damages, including but not limited to special, incidental, consequential, or other damages. Readers should be aware that Internet websites offered as citations and/or sources for further information may have changed or disappeared between the time this was written and when it is read.

ISBN 978-66782-728-5 (pbk.) ISBN # 978-66782-729-2 (ebk.)

Printed in the United States of America

For Diana, who encouraged me to get these thoughts on paper. Thank you for your patience, suggestions, and support. Couldn't do this without you.

And for Adrian and Isaac. I'm so very proud of you.

And for anyone who was thrown into the deep end of the virtual delivery pool – I feel your pain.

Table of Contents

Introduction

At the beginning of 2020, most people had never even heard the word "webinar" or had much experience with virtual learning.

And then COVID-19 happened.

Suddenly everyone was thrown into virtual meeting rooms faster than you could say "You're on mute". Whether people wanted them or not, virtual meetings and online training sessions were dumped on them. And we now know they're here to stay!

By now, we've all had nearly two years to experience the good, the bad and the downright ugly in online sessions. So now, when they're invited to yet another online learning event or meeting, a lot of people think **"Not Another F*cking Webinar!!"**

One of the legacies of the COVID-19 pandemic is the impact of digitization on businesses as they were forced to pivot to online models due to the shift in consumer needs and habits. Having an online presence went from being a bonus to an absolute necessity. Because of COVID-19, the world of training has changed—forever. Global pandemics have a way of doing that. Over the past year and a half, thousands of trainers, presenters, and teachers have been forced to move their lessons online. In addition, hundreds of thousands of employees were forced to work from home— staying connected to teams and co-workers virtually, using anything they had on hand. Many who would have never been exposed to e-learning or the virtual space have been suddenly forced to get online.

This has been both a blessing and a curse for webinar presenters.

Online sessions make it easier to present learning in smaller bite-sized chunks and just as easy to make the learning dull, lifeless, and utterly useless for the learner. Virtual delivery has proven to be effective during this pandemic, so even after we eliminate the COVID-19 risk, virtual delivery will continue to be an important part of every organization's training and development plan going forward in this recalibrated learning environment.

Whether you're a teacher, sales trainer, or team lead who hosts an occasional online meeting, or you're a regular webinar host delivering multiple online training sessions every month, it's now more important than ever to make sure you deliver the most professional webinar possible because virtual delivery is **not going away.** If anything, we're just getting started.

This book will lead you through the common mistakes that stand in the way of delivering an exceptional learning experience. One key idea I'd like to share is about giving an **"ARM and a LEG"** to your participants and yourself.

If you think back to music concerts you might have attended pre-pandemic, they always involve your favourite band or singer, and that concert features a lot of your favorite songs. For the performers on the stage, this may have been the two-thousandth time they've played that number. But every time they sing it, it comes across as genuine and meant only for you, right? Because professional performers (and that's what you are aspiring to be in the virtual arena) give 110% for every performance. They're prepared to lay it all out there for their audience—and so should you! So, I've created a simple, easy-to-remember, and powerful formula for you to use to make sure your webinar comes across as the "best concert" your attendees have attended.

Before I get started on that, below are some comments from virtual sessions held over the past many months that have been shared with me.

"The session was a complete waste of time." Franck S.
"The content was good, but the presenter tried to pack too much into the time we had. I feel we skipped over things too fast." Lorne W.
"I got kicked out of the audio channel when we went to a breakout room and the audio didn't return when we got back. I tried reconnecting twice but gave up to do some real work." Carol T.
"Glad this was only a 2-hour session. I can't imagine spending a full day with this presenter." Rupinder K.
"After three failed attempts I gave up trying to log into the session. Invest in better technology!" Anonymous

Most virtual sessions leave a lot to be desired—lousy graphics, too much top–down teaching, no interactions with fellow attendees, tons of theory but no practical application—in short, a big waste of time for everyone, facilitator, and participants alike.

Why has the webinar degenerated into this time suck in such a short time span?

Here are a few reasons.

- Hundreds of people were forced into the virtual arena without proper training or any idea about how different virtual delivery is from face-to-face delivery.

- Many companies, organizations, and academic institutions were forced to pivot quickly during the global pandemic and change up the way they train or sell. That panic to move into the virtual space didn't give their people much time to learn the nuances of virtual delivery. As a result, people with little or no experience in the virtual space were thrown into the deep end of the pool and most came up sputtering.

- Most were also thrown into entirely new technology spaces—having to learn programs like WebEx or Teams or Zoom, relying on headsets or earbuds, working from home, trimming a full day learning event into a few hours or less on the Internet.

- As their experience in the virtual space grew, many began to realize they were still trying to cram "eight pounds of spuds into a five-pound bag," as my grandmother used to say, because they thought they needed all the content from the live session to be included in the virtual one. In the end, what they were delivering wasn't landing and wasn't translating into learning for the attendees.

I'm Dale Nelson, and years before the rest of the world was forced to embrace platforms like Adobe Connect, Zoom, or Cisco WebEx, I was crafting and delivering virtual learning experiences to clients from around the world. I've had the opportunity to use or test a variety of webinar platforms and become familiar with some of their quirks as well as some of their advantages. Since 2015, I've been delivering online webinars every month to people from all walks of life.

Over the past decade, I've compiled a notebook of just about every mistake you can make in the virtual space, and nearly everything that can go wrong—*because I've probably made those mistakes or had those things go sideways on me during a session*.

I've also assembled a list of Pro Tips I'll share in this book as well as my "ARM and a LEG" principles, which I've developed to ensure virtual sessions deliver maximum value to everyone—participants, sponsors, and you!

So, let's get going. The sooner we start, the sooner you're going to be a webinar professional!

Chapter 1 – The switch to virtual

It wasn't supposed to be this way.

Companies had training rooms, annual sales conferences, regional team meetings, and numerous other opportunities for employees to meet, collaborate, and learn together. Entire departments were devoted to sourcing venues, lining up keynote speakers, preparing agendas and putting together entertaining, engaging, and expensive events.

And then, a global pandemic happened!

Almost everyone has had a taste of this new virtual learning and meeting environment we've been forced into because of a worldwide pandemic. Parents have attended parent–teacher interviews via Zoom. Employees have attended team and company meetings via Teams, WebEx, Google Hangouts, or a dozen other virtual platforms. By now, surely everyone knows what to expect, how to use the various controls, mute themselves, and handle their webcam, right?

Sadly, even though we may all be more familiar with using many of the virtual tools available to us than we were a couple years ago, there's still a learning curve to deal with. Unlike a meeting room where you can just open your mouth and be heard, this new virtual arena requires us to learn a few things. How many times have you heard "You're on mute" over the past couple years?

Just like learning the controls of a new car, every time you get into the seat of a virtual workshop, there are probably a few buttons and adjustments you're not familiar with. As a facilitator or producer of a virtual event, it's your first job to make sure everyone knows where things are.

Think back to when you could do this training in the boardroom or a classroom. What were some of the first housekeeping items to get answered?

- Where are the washrooms?
- When will we stop for breaks?
- Can you interrupt me along the way with a question, or is it best to make a note and we'll deal with it in the Q & A at the end of the session?
- What happens if you are interrupted and need to step out of the class for a few minutes?

Just like the old brick-and-mortar training room, you need to get these basic housekeeping items out of the way first thing.

You're probably not going to be able to provide directions to the washroom, but you can certainly let folks know the anticipated outcomes for the session.

What are your expectations as a facilitator? Do you want them to interrupt you or save their questions for pre-planned breaks? Can they unmute themselves or do you need them to raise their hand to speak?

Lay all this out in advance.

You also need to provide them with the necessary tips and tricks for the virtual platform you're using. While a lot of the features are the same from one program to another, each virtual platform is laid out just a little different—like those gauges and buttons in a new car—and it's your first task to make sure everyone knows where to find things.

As an example, here are some of the slides I use in my opening "Lobby Deck" when using Zoom. Other platforms have slightly different slides, but you get the idea.

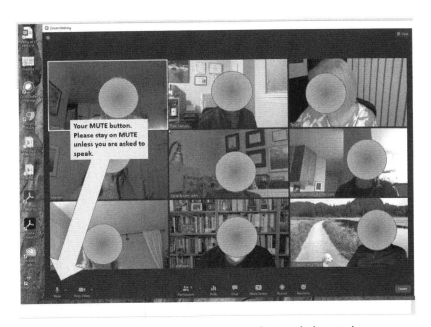

Show attendees where the mute button is located.

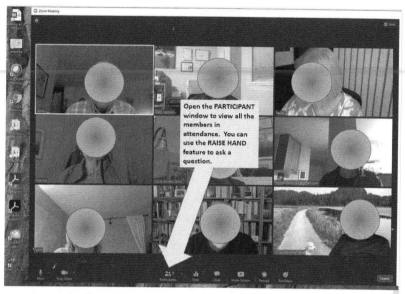

Indicate where the participant window link is.

Show where the Chat function button is located.

Before I start with the main content of the session, I spend the first two or three minutes making sure everyone understands where the various controls are, and what platform features we will be using throughout the session. This is also the perfect time to pre-answer some of those questions attendees have when they show up. While the graphic is up on the screen, you've got the opportunity to show participants where the various controls are located so they can mute themselves, raise a hand to ask questions, provide feedback in the chat window, and so forth.

The images shown earlier illustrate a great example of using the same slide but adding different elements as you go about introducing the various features of the webinar program. Instead of having people stare at the same image while you describe where the controls are, add visual elements that help direct their eye to the correct spot. Show them—don't tell them.

Pro Tip

Grab a screenshot of your virtual platform's welcome page or landing page. You can do this by logging in as a participant and capturing the image of what a participant will see when they log into your session using a snipping tool or screen grab. There are lots of image editing programs you can use, both paid and open source, which will allow you to create a slide in your deck that provides a visual clue to where folks can find the various items you'll be using in your session.

In the example above, I've simply just dropped it into a PowerPoint slide and used some of the drawing features available in the program to create arrows that point to various controls and dropped a text box onto the image to explain what that control does.

You can have a few of these slides in your "lobby deck" to show people where the controls are for things like polls, reactions, chat, and so forth. It's far easier than trying to explain everything to everyone.

A picture really IS worth a thousand words, so use an image to highlight your programs controls and features.

Chapter 2 – Webinars done right

You might be tempted to say, "It's just another training session, right? How hard can this be?" You've done this lots of times in the physical training room space, so moving to a virtual platform shouldn't require a lot of over-thinking. Right?

Wrong!

What worked in the physical training room **might** still work in the virtual space, but chances are there's a lot you're going to have to change.

The room

First – the obvious.

You're not in the same room as the attendees. Exactly why does this matter? For one thing, you've only got your voice and very little body language to accompany the session.

A typical Zoom layout with participant faces

That little video window attendees see really doesn't capture the entirety of your personality like being physically in front of the group does. They may be able to see your gestures but you're not going to be able to walk around the room like in the physical space. For many presenters, this feels like they are being handcuffed to their chair as this reduces their ability to physically engage the audience. Some presenters are noted for walking around the entire audience, engaging them with stories, drawing real life examples from the attendees, physically making themselves a part of the audience.

You can still do this is the virtual space, but it takes a little practice, and you'll need to perfect your "close-up" moments as they say in the movie business. How do you do this? By paying attention to a few critical components.

Your audio

Even professional performers learn to adapt. Think about singers who work a quieter set of songs into their routine. They may even pull out a tall stool and sit, playing an acoustic guitar, instead of moving around the stage. They're still able to capture the audience's attention and deliver their message – but without the stage antics. They're using their voice and their music to keep you engaged and connected to the performance.

And you've got your voice to work with, so you must make it work for you.

Be sure you're speaking clearly. Avoid "horse feathers" as my childhood elocution teacher taught me—those useless sounds we make when we're talking, such as "aah" or "um" or "like." If you want to know if you're using horse feathers, sit down with the recorder app on your phone, or a small recording device, and record yourself.

Work from your presentation script and record about five to ten minutes of your presentation. Then, listen back with a critical ear to catch if you're dropping these useless phrases or sounds into your speech. If you are, now is the time to practice dropping them.

Rerecord the same piece keeping in mind your new awareness of some of those speech "tics" many of us employ. Re-listen and keep polishing that presentation until those horse feathers are a thing of the past.

Instead of making these sounds, learn to let the silence happen. It's easier for the participants to tolerate a second or two of silence as you move from one thought to another than it is to constantly hear an "um" or "aah." I once sat in on a session where the horse feathers were so thick, I gave up actively listening to what was being said and started keeping score of the number of interruptions. I got all the way to thirty-two before the session ended and I honestly can't say I got anything out of the webinar other than what an aggravating habit the presenter had.

Another important reason to record a lengthy piece of your session is to listen for things like pace and wording. I've sat in on several virtual sessions where the presenter really wasn't aware of just how fast they were speaking. Their cadence, coupled with a regional or local accent for example, made it a real strain for participants to keep up.

I worked for some time with an organization head-quartered in Scotland with team members all around the world. It was not uncommon for folks to interrupt a presenter from head office to ask them to slow down a bit—the speed of their words coupled with a thick Scottish brogue was too hard for non-English speakers to properly understand (and many of us who do speak English found it difficult too.)

This is an important consideration for presenters who use English as a second language. If you are presenting in English, remember your accent and cadence may make it more difficult for attendees to understand your message, so speak slower than you might normally and often check for understanding. Be prepared to rephrase or reword things if the message isn't landing the way you want it to.

Keep your audience in mind, particularly if you're working across globally dispersed teams or organizations. Regional words and phrases might cause confusion for some listeners. For example, in North America, we might call the vehicle horses are transported in a "horse trailer"; in parts of Europe the same thing is called a "horse box." What you refer to as the "trunk" of your car someone else may call a "boot." One person's "slippers" are another's "house shoes."

These are just examples of how regionalized words and

phrases can end up sounding odd or off-putting to some attendees. Just because we may all be speaking English doesn't mean we're using the same English words and phrases. When possible, avoid them or at least be prepared to provide an appropriate translation.

Recording yourself on a regular basis will give you the opportunity to hear what your participants hear—and if YOU find something you don't like, chances are your audience will too. So, practice delivering the session slower, or with a more varied pace. Slow down for the critical lesson pieces so you're not skating over the salient points. You'll have time to speed up at other parts of the presentation. And don't forget to vary the pitch and volume of your voice throughout the presentation. No one wants to hear a monotone for an entire session.

Recording yourself gives you the chance to make sure you're emphasising the correct word in each sentence. And changing the emphatic word can make a huge difference on what your audience will hear. For example, let's look at the following sentence and simply change the word we're emphasizing. Depending on where we're putting our voice, the entire sentence, and its meaning changes.

I did not call him a liar.

I did **not** call him a liar.

I did not **call** him a liar.

I did not call **him** a liar.

I did not call him a **liar.**

Try reading each line with emphasis on the bolded word.

I had the advantage of working in the radio industry for many years, but you don't need to be a trained voice actor or professional announcer to benefit from recording and listening to your presentation with an ear to making it better. You're trying to polish your presentation to deliver the best session possible.

Even if you can't be on camera during your webinar, make sure your face is showing emotions and feelings as you speak, and that will come through in your voice. If you're smiling, your audience will "hear" it. If you're excited and happy to share something, then that will come through in the tone and pace of what you're saying. Your voice is the most important tool you have in the webinar room, so really pay attention to that. Remember to emphasize on important words or phrases in your presentation—raise your voice or slow down for a dramatic effect. It adds impact and memorability to what you're saying.

Attire

Dress for the event. Even though it's virtual, showing up in baggy sweatpants and a T-shirt will undermine your professionalism. Believe it or not, it wasn't that long ago that radio announcers for the English BBC network who delivered the six o'clock evening news were contractually obligated to **wear a dinner jacket**—even though they were on radio!

In the 1920s, the powers-that-be at the BBC deemed the evening news **so essential** and that specific time slot **so important** they insisted the delivery be polished and professional. They believed if the announcer was suitably attired – dressed for a formal dinner - they would take the job of delivering the news with the dignity and formality it deserved.

Pro Tip

Take a selfie and ask yourself, "Would I wear this to an in-person event?"

Attendance sheets

One of the big differences between live and virtual events

is your use of the attendance sheet. In a live session, you basically check off people as they come into the room and that's the end of it. The sheet is only used to track attendance and report back to the sponsor or organizer on who showed up for the event.

In virtual rooms, the attendance sheet becomes a vital piece of the session. You're going to use it to keep track of who attended, sure. But it should be used for so much more.

Leave room for notes; during your "waiting room" or lobby session, or during your ice breaker exercise, you've got the chance to learn about each attendee. Capture the details and statements by those who are entering the session.

- Sarah loves dogs.
- Troy is new to his role.
- Agnes has been in the same company for 14 years.
- Raj is a new parent.
- Alan just bought a house.

All this is powerful information to have at your fingertips during the session. Write down any details you can discover about each participant without being bothersome or intrusive. Some folks will be naturally chatty and offer up lots of personal insight. Others will be reluctant to share and will need encouragement. Be sociable to everyone and chances are they'll respond in kind.

Learn to pronounce names correctly by asking if you

must—it's important to be able to call people by their name and not inadvertently offend them because you can't pronounce it. If you do encounter a name you are unfamiliar with, don't be afraid to admit you need help pronouncing it. You might say something like "Hi, Latisha—am I pronouncing that right?" If you get corrected, make a note on the attendance sheet, and write the name phonetically—La-THEA-sha, or La-THI-Sha, for example. Then, for the rest of the session, you don't have to worry about getting the pronunciation correct.

Globally dispersed teams are often multicultural in nature so the chance of having people with names you're unfamiliar with is very high. Make every effort in working with your session sponsor or team lead to establish exactly who will be attending your session and where in the world they're located. In addition, remember, the more dispersed the team, the greater likelihood of having folks with English as a second language. You may need to rethink how your presentation is going to be delivered to give those who speak another language the opportunity to get the full value from the session.

In today's dispersed workforce, it's not uncommon to have team members distributed across multiple time-zones, too. This can create unique problems in making sure your invitations are crafted to reflect the start time of your session in the participant's time zone. There are numerous resources you can access via the web, but the simplest are often baked into the webinar software you choose. Check to be certain an event set up for your time-zone will automatically adjust to the local time-zone of those you invite to your session.

Participants

Determining your audience mix is important too. The world is made up of introverts and extroverts, and your webinar session will probably have some of both.

In his work, Psychological Types, the Swiss psychiatrist and psychoanalyst Carl Jung identified four major personality types, so prepare for some of each in your webinar rooms. Jung differentiated people according to their general attitude, which he described as *"a person's way of reacting to outer and inner experiences."* He named and distinguished these attitudes as Introversion and Extroversion. Introverted types tend to be quieter, inwardly focused, thoughtful, and cautions. Extroverted types tend to be more talkative, outwardly focused, outspoken, and bold.

Jung then went on to classify people as either "head" persons—those who prefer to make decisions by thinking things through, and what he called "heart" persons, those who prefer to evaluate subjectively using what he called the "feeling" function. The thinking types appear more formal, analytical, detached, and task-focused while the "feeling" types tend to appear more informal, instinctive, involved, and relationship-focused.

So, you're going to have a combination of all four basic types in your room: the Introverted Feeling type, the

Introverted Thinking type, the Extroverted Feeling type, and the Extroverted Thinking type. Knowing this, you can design your session to provide the right content for all four basic types. And you'll also be prepared to recognize those extroverts and introverts who require a little more data (those "head person" thinking types) from those who are more instinctive in their learning ("heart person" feeling types). You're not going to type everyone correctly but planning for each of these four personality types goes a long way in making sure your content resonates with everyone.

And remember, you'll need to "show up" as each of these four personality types as well to meet the participant "where they live." You'll need to become comfortable stepping out of your own comfort zone from time to time to adapt and connect with your audience.

With a little experience, you'll soon be able to get an impression of whether your attendee is more of an introvert or more an extrovert. This can be helpful because you may have to coax a comment out of the introverts while the extroverts rarely need encouragement to speak up. In fact, you might have to tactfully ask some folks to allow others some time on the microphone as some people will take time to formulate their answer. Introverts usually "think to speak" whereas extroverts are the type who "speak to think." With extroverts, it's not unusual for you and them to hear their idea for the first time together—it's just said out loud. Introverts tend to want to think about their response first, so don't rush them for a comment or input.

Make a note of any characteristics you sense during the welcome session on your attendance sheet.

Are they shy?

Do they sound outgoing and eager?

Is English perhaps their second language?

Keeping track of all this information is important as you work your way through your presentation. Being able to call on someone, or encourage them to contribute, helps keep engagement up and involves all participants in the learning experience.

It's unlikely you'll have to use preferred pronouns during your webinar, but this is an important consideration in today's virtual world. Knowing whether to refer to a participant as he/him or she/her or they/them might be important, so be sure to work that question into some of your pre-work or your webinar invitation. Asking for preferred pronouns is becoming much more common, and it adds to your professionalism. You probably won't need to refer to participants by their preferred pronoun, but if you need to, you'll have them.

Another point to remember is that although you may be addressing a group of people try to keep "an audience of one" in mind as you go through your material. Avoid using group terms like "company" or "team" or "you all" and instead keep your presentation in the singular with terms like "you" and "yours." Take a page from professional radio announcers who imagine one singular listener tuned into their broadcast.

Keeping the presentation focused on an audience of one will set you up to better connect with every participant because it will sound as though you're speaking to them directly.

Session content

That PowerPoint slide deck with 181 slides you used in the face-to-face session—that needs to go. (See Chapter 6 for PowerPoint tips and ideas)

Those bullet points that you read verbatim—get rid of them!

If that's the material you need to cover and it all needs to be in the presentation, maybe just consider emailing the slide deck to participants so they can read it themselves. That saves you the time and trouble of delivering the session and saves them a lot of aggravation.

In the virtual room, you don't get that same direct feedback. Even if your participants are on a webcam, those little one-inch images don't provide the same subtle feedback as a live session, so you need to check for engagement in other ways. And you need to make sure your presentation can hold their attention.

Pro Tip

Don't read slides verbatim. Paraphrase or reword your speaking notes, so you're not just reading aloud to attendees. This isn't story time.

Most of your participants can read just as well as you so don't make the mistake of reading everything that's on the screen.

Another thing to remember is that in the virtual space, there is no consistency in the way participants are connecting to or accessing your webinar

In the physical room, everyone is getting the same screen view; they share similar seating and so on. In the virtual space, it's not the same. Some folks will be using a Window-based computer and others will be on their Mac or even a tablet or cell phone. Some will be seated in their home office, while others are joining from their kitchen chair or even their sofa. Some folks will have lots of experience in using the technology at their fingertips and others may be less fluent. You need to find a way of levelling this playing field so everyone gets a great webinar experience regardless of the technology that might get in the way.

Taking a couple minutes at the start of the session helps set the stage for a great experience for everyone.

As I mentioned before, one thing I really recommend is creating a "lobby deck" or a set of welcoming slides that precede your actual presentation. For example, you might want to have a screenshot of the tech platform you're using, outlining where the various controls are located. You may want to display any telephone numbers associated with the session for those who must dial into the audio channel or have difficulty with their computer audio setup.

I've found some of the tools associated with Adobe Connect very useful. There's a starting time timer you can install, which counts down to the start time of the session.

Adobe Connect Countdown-to-session start timer.

This is a great way of letting people know that you're going to start at a certain time, and they won't have to stare at a blank welcome screen. Other platforms offer different features, so it's important to find a webinar software program that works for you. If you're comfortable using it, it's going to be easier to get your participants on board too.

Another thing you can consider doing is adding a music feed or MP3 feed with some generic "lobby" music that plays and allows folks to preconfigure their audio feed for the session. It's also a good way to let people know they've dialed into a live session—there's nothing worse than wondering whether you're in the right virtual room because you can't hear anything, and the slide you're looking at seems frozen on some generic welcome message.

One note of caution on this: Often, the MP3 player or sound source used to provide a music track in the lobby isn't the same as the audio feed your participants will use when they want to hear you or speak up. Make sure your audio channel is live in advance of the session. There's nothing more frustrating that wasting the first five minutes of a session fiddling around with sound settings.

If you choose to create a lobby deck, be sure to keep it short and visual. **Show** people; don't tell them. Create a graphic using a screenshot of the platform with arrows indicating the various controls like in the example below.

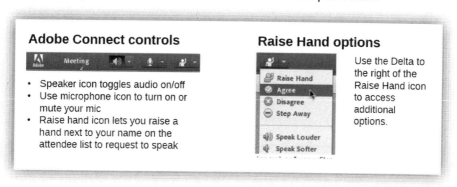

An example of an Adobe Connect session user menu used in a welcome presentation or lobby deck.

It's easy for people to see where the controls are when they have a visual aide; telling them the "Chat" is the far-left button down at the bottom of the screen doesn't convey the same information and may leave some attendees confused.

As I said before, when in doubt, show them.

Using a cohost or producer

If you're working with a producer or cohost for your

session, be sure to connect well in advance to compare notes and exchange any information you have on the session. You don't want your partner having to scramble to catch up to what the session is about, and you certainly don't want to be inserting something unexpected into the presentation if you haven't already discussed it.

Setting things up in advance lets you script out what will be happening and who oversees making it happen. Knowing in advance that a certain poll needs to be pulled up, or a breakout room is assembled and ready for action can help move the webinar along and keep the action lively for everyone.

Working with a co-host or producer also allows you to concentrate on the attendees without having to constant check on what is happening in the Chat window or who may have raised their hand to ask a question. Having help on sessions can be a real benefit, so if you have the chance to work with someone on your webinar, do so.

Chapter 3 – An ARM and a LEG

The "Godfather of Soul" James Brown *(1933–2006)* also earned the reputation of "the hardest working man in show-business." Brown started singing in church groups as a kid and worked his way up to becoming one of the most influential figures in twentieth century popular music.

Not only did he perform thousands of shows, but he also kept up his grueling concert schedule in his later years even as he fought prostate cancer. His lawyer Jay Ross said Brown would routinely "lose two or three pounds each time he performed" because he was that physical on-stage. He left it all out there for his audience. Now, that's delivering!

Brown was also an obsessive perfectionist, which made his backup band miserable, but that insistence on perfection made his group sound tight as a drum and resulted in some of the most memorable songs ever recorded. His focus on perfection and his insistence on delivering everything he and his band could give at every performance earned him a loyal following and the respect of the entire music industry.

Now what does this little story have to do with your webinar delivery?

Everything.

As a professional, you need to commit to deliver an "**ARM and a LEG"** for every webinar session **you** host or present. I'm not suggesting you need to sweat off two or three pounds each session, but you DO need to put everything and more into creating a professional experience for your attendees.

So, what do I mean when I say an ARM and a LEG? Merriam-Webster defines "an arm and a leg" as "a very large amount of money," and explains it further with a sample sentence, *"It's a reliable car, and it doesn't cost an arm and a leg."* This means that the investment you make isn't unreasonable. What I'm saying is that every webinar you "invest" in **should** involve a substantial amount of time and effort invested by you.

You need to give participants an "ARM and a LEG" in every session you deliver:

Applicable

Relevant

Memorable

Lean

Engaging

Genuine

ARM and a LEG

Let's examine the ARM and LEG in greater detail.

ARM = Applicable - Relevant - Memorable

APPLICABLE

Merriam-Webster defines "Applicable" as an adjective, meaning "capable of or suitable for being applied; Appropriate." Ask yourself—is what the participant takes away applicable for their business challenge? Is it the best tool for them to use in this case? Is it appropriate?

How do you make sure your participants are finding the application in your session, not just the information? Unless they can translate the content into practical application immediately following the webinar, the session has been a waste of time for you both.

Prior to the session—before you even begin to design your slide deck and organize your learning objectives—you need to determine what the participant wants to take away from your session. You can gain this information talking with the session sponsor or the head of the department arranging the session. If you're a sales manager preparing a session for your sales team, keep in mind the various strengths and personalities of each of your team members. If you're a teacher prepping for a lesson, keep each of those students front and centre while you're designing your session—not all learn at the same pace, and some may need to hear the material presented in a different fashion before they completely understand.

If you are unable to get this advance intelligence about your upcoming audience, then be sure to make the most of that "pre-session" time in the lobby or waiting room with them. (See Attendance Sheets in the previous chapter.) Try to gather as much insight into who is in the virtual room with you so you can be clear on making the session something they can apply as soon as it concludes. The sooner they can apply the material into their real lives, the more likely it will stick in long-term memory.

Make sure to provide some pre-work for your session; use this to also collect each participant's reason for attending the session. If you know why they're in the webinar room, it's not that difficult to make sure they take away what they need.

Unless you first understand their reason for attending, it will be impossible to create a learning session they can apply immediately. And you want them to be able to apply the concepts or ideas as soon as possible after the webinar—having them wait weeks or months before using the learning just doesn't work as they're just not going to be able to remember the content unless they're able to apply it immediately.

RELEVANT

Another adjective, as per Merriam Webster meaning "having significant and demonstrable bearing on the matter at hand." Other definitions include "affording evidence tending to prove or disprove the matter at issue or under discussion," or "having social relevance."

There's no point in loading up your presentation with a bunch of real-life examples if they don't translate to your audience. If you're going to relate the material to the participants, it needs to be in terms they can understand and relate to.

I once attended a session where the presenter focused on some specific accounting functions of a particular software program. They detailed how to create graphs and charts to express the spreadsheet data. They offered ideas and suggestions, but the information didn't land with half the audience because we were not directly engaged in financial reporting.

While the content of the session was solid, it was only valuable and relevant to those who were directly working in the accounting function of the organization. For the rest of us, it wasn't information we needed at that time. I did learn something, and continue to use the program in some situations, but the session didn't pack the punch it could have because the content wasn't relevant to me.

Again, knowing who is in your room and what <u>they</u> hope to take away from the session allows you to design something that is relevant for every attendee.

MEMORABLE

An adjective, which means "worth remembering" or "easily remembered, especially because of being special or unusual." How memorable is the content of your session? How is it special or unusual? What sets it apart from the myriad of resources available elsewhere?

Researchers[1] tell us there are four kinds of memory: Sensory, Short-term, Working, and Long-Term.

Sensory memory is very brief (about three seconds) recall of a sensory experience, such as what we just saw or heard. Think of sensory memory as a quick snapshot of something you've just experienced that quickly fades away.

Short-term memory is where you can recall information you were just exposed to. This might be anywhere from thirty seconds to a few days, depending on the situation. Short-term memory is often tasked when you're running up the stairs to get something, only to get to the top and wonder why you ran up there. What was I looking for? Why did I come up here? It's not forgetfulness—it's just your brain wrestling with that file cabinet we call memory.

Working memory is often defined as the ability of our brains to keep a limited amount of information available long enough to use it. One example might be cramming for an exam or pulling ideas together for a presentation you're making. Working memory helps process thoughts and plans, as well as carries out ideas. But once the exam is over, or the

---

[1] See 4 Types of Memory: Sensory, Short Term, Working & Long Term at https://www.verywellhealth.com/types-of-memory-explained-98552

presentation is done, the information we've stored in our memory fades away. How much do you honestly remember from that chemistry final in high school? Unless you're working in the medical field, there's a pretty good chance what you considered "necessary" at one point is long gone right now.

Long-term memory encompasses memories that range from a few days to decades. For successful learning to take place, information needs to move from the sensory or short-term memory to long-term memory. To make that to happen, you need to make the idea "sticky" enough that it's easy to remember because it's easy to retain and recall. Crafting your presentation with the idea of generating long-term effect on your participants is a key component of developing a professional webinar that creates results.

One example of sticky technique I use is when I'm introduced to people. My name is Dale, but I let folks know DALE is really an acronym for "Do A Little Extra". This helps anchor my name correctly into their memory and I'm rarely mistakenly called Dave or Darryl after that. It is sticky enough people remember, and that's what you want to weave into your presentation.

Think of ways to make your material "sticky" for folks— they'll remember it long after the session and that's the aim of the game. Keeping the learning alive by keeping it in long-term memory is what we're trying to achieve here.

LEG = Lean - Engaging - Genuine

LEAN

If you look at most professional athletes, their body-mass index is pretty low. They're not packing a lot of extra weight around (with the possible exception of line backers and Sumo wrestlers, and even then, there's a lot of muscle under there). The same should be true of your webinar—you don't want it containing a bunch of "fluff" or irrelevant material. You want to trim the fat from your presentation and keep it as lean as possible.

Keep your presentation focused on the key learning objectives and make sure your participant outcomes are front-and-centre to help ensure success.

I come back to the slide deck again—in most cases, less is more. You don't have to have 150 slides in your presentation when 50 slides with lots of activity and key concepts will do. While you don't want to leave the same slide up there for minutes on end, you also don't want thirty slides that basically say the same things in different fonts.

Perhaps consider instead of trying to pack everything into one two-hour session, create two ninety-minute events that cover the same material. Participants won't be overwhelmed by idea-upon-idea, and you'll have the ability to really anchor the key concepts from the first session by repeating and building on them in a second session that offers a deeper dive into the material.

ENGAGING

The more inter-active and engaging your session can be, the greater the likelihood your participants will remain focused and participating in their learning. How much engagement are you consciously building into your presentation?

- What ice breakers are you going to use?
- What questions are you going to ask?
- Are you structuring polls or chat feedbacks?
- What sort of peer-to-peer exchanges are you building in?

What activities do you have planned for your attendees? Are you going to ask them to draw on the whiteboard, or take notes via the text tool?

Engaging with your participants starts well before the session. You've got opportunities to connect pre-webinar with pre-work, pre-session expectation exploration, eye-appealing invitations, and so on. The more you can connect ahead of the actual webinar, the less likely folks show up considering you a stranger—you've already had several communications or connections with them in the time leading up to the session.

You don't have to have hundreds of slides in your presentation—it's probably best not to. Instead, keep the presentation lean and find ways to overlay your slide with a poll or white board for additional depth and discussion. Get participants involved in the presentation by asking them to notate or comment in the space you've provided. The slide in the background won't have to change but the dialogue and exchange happening on the screen will become the focus and keep people engaged.

On the day of the webinar, be sure you're in the room early. No one likes to show up to a session before the host— and the time you invest in the waiting room or lobby really pays off as you get to chat one-to-one with attendees as they arrive.

Make every effort to keep your web camera on and look directly at it when speaking to participants. (See more on webcams in Chapter 11)

Unless there is a technical issue from preventing your use of a web cam, it's always a good idea to be on camera. People like to see who they're interacting with, and you're missing an opportunity to connect on a more personal level if you're just a disembodied voice on the other side of that computer screen.

Two other "E" words to remember when building an engaging session are "excitement" and "enthusiasm." What excitement can you weave into your presentation? Are you excited to be a part of the session or are you just going through the motions? Are you 'contagious' about the material?

How eager do you sound? People can hear if you're not passionate about what you're delivering, so don't get complacent with this audience.

GENUINE

The French novelist Jean Giraudoux *(1882–1944)* once jokingly remarked, *"The secret of success is sincerity. Once you can fake that, you've got it made."* When you think about it, you can really hear whether a presenter is truly committed to delivering a session, or whether they're "faking" their way through the presentation.

The Phantom of the Opera is the longest running Broadway show in history, with over 13,300 performances. It premiered on January 26, 1988 and is still playing at the Majestic Theatre in New York (resumed October 2021)—that's over thirty years!

Ticket holders still get a unique personalized experience, thanks to the professional cast and crew. They may have played the part for hundreds of shows, and yet when they take to the stage, their performance comes straight from the heart. They're not faking it. They're not lip-syncing. They're genuinely enjoying the show as much as you are because they love what they do—and you can hear the sincerity and spontaneity in their performance. The character they're playing and the world they're creating on-stage is a little different each time because of who may be sitting in the rows beyond the stage lights, and they build on that to deliver a once-in-a-lifetime experience for their audience every time.

In your webinar, show you genuinely care about the people in attendance. Start from the very beginning by learning their names, jotting down any notes or observations (make use of that attendance list*)*, and really reach out to connect with every single participant. When your attendees hear the sincerity in your voice, they will maintain their focus on the content—and you'll be perceived as genuinely caring and concerned for their session outcomes.

One simple way to make sure you're coming across as genuine is to constantly "be in the moment" of your webinar. This takes practice, but you don't want to be thinking about other things when you're delivering. Stay focused on your participants and keep the session lively and engaging. This means you need to practice using your webinar software to the point you're not stumbling around trying to solve a technical issue and losing the focus on your session. If you're calm and relaxed during the session that will come through to your audience, and they'll hear how genuine you are.

What's your "special sauce" or "hook"?

Can you think of an acronym to use with your name?

Do you have a hobby or something interesting you can share with those in the room? You're trying to connect human to human here—so, don't be afraid to share some personal details along the way.

What is your competitive advantage? Why should people pay attention to what you're saying?

There are lots of resources out there, so what sets YOUR webinar apart? It only needs to be one thing, but that becomes your USP and that's what you can build a professional webinar career on.

Chapter 4 – Why virtual?

Let's look at some of the pros and cons of virtual delivery.

Pros include the following:

- Affordability
- Ease of access
- Efficiency
- Increased quality of learning material

Saving money is a big plus if you are working on improving and advancing your professional development. Getting a degree online can be a lot faster and easier than taking the traditional route.

One of the biggest advantages of a virtual session is people can attend from anywhere around the world—from their office or the comfort of their own home. I've had sessions where attendees admitted they were still in their bedroom slippers—they told me. They didn't feel the need to get all dressed up to attend a session in their own living room.

Travel is another issue—it can be expensive to attend training. By the time you book flights, hotel rooms, transportation to and from the airport, meals and so forth, it can really add up. Not to mention sleeping in a strange bed, eating hotel or room service food, time away from family or friends, and generally losing a few days of "normal," live events take a toll. Virtual sessions eliminate the travel expense and inconveniences altogether.

Virtual sessions are often followed up with additional digital learning resources. Unlike a take-away textbook or participant program from a live session, these are digital resources participants can access on their own time, when they want them. This can help anchor the learning and keep the learning alive long after the virtual session is over. You might consider working with your session sponsor to create some pre-recorded bite-sized videos or PowerPoint recordings to reinforce the contents of your webinar which participants can access later.

Some live sessions are consciously moving into this virtual "follow-up" space, but it's taking time. And many of these follow-up sessions feel like they're being added because that's what the audience is demanding, rather than delivering something of real value. If you're going to go down this route, be sure you're adding value for your participants and not simply repeating the content from your session.

Virtual learning fits nicely into today's working style for most people. We like a combination of learning opportunities, and virtual sessions are usually shorter, more bite-sized opportunities for development. This can really give folks the gift of time as they don't have to commit to an entire day of training session but perhaps only an hour or two. They don't even have to spend commuting time getting to your workshop. These shorter virtual sessions really act as a sort of "micro learning" for folks who now can tap into learning resources **as they need them.**

In short, virtual sessions provide real convenience for the learner, putting the session "where they live."

But it's not all unicorns and pixie dust. There are disadvantages to virtual delivery too.

Cons include the following:

- Technology issues
- Less social interaction
- Reputation
- Specialized education is limited for now

Failing technology is the biggest stumbling block (see Chapter 11 for a deeper dive into technology troubles). For now, it's important to remember that the virtual world really depends on stable, reliable technology. There are a lot of moving parts here, from your choice of webinar software right on through to the attendee's internet connection, the web browser they use, even the type of device they use to connect to your session.

There are a growing number of webinar software programs available, and this creates its own set of problems. Learners can sometimes be overwhelmed by the sheer number of platforms there are to learn and navigate. Although they all do basically the same thing, the way they're set up and where the various controls are located all vary from program to program. It's important to remember to include a short technology overview at the beginning of your session for those that may be using your system for the first time.

Another drawback to virtual is ensuring participants get enough feedback and support in the session. This lack of in person verbal communication coupled with the fact you can't really see the participants to gauge their level of engagement can create a real disconnect between the facilitator and the participants.

One thing missing from virtual sessions are the social interactions that normally take place in a F2F room. Gathering by the coffee machine during breaks or stepping out into the hallway to grab a little one-to-one time with coworkers or new acquaintances is a big part of live sessions. And that's all lost in the virtual arena, so you need to make space for these sorts of exchanges by using things like breakout rooms and chat.

That said, there are learners who find the virtual space more comfortable than a classroom. While social interactions can be critical for some, it can be a real burden for others. (I'm talking to you, introverts.) Most of the time, they will feel pressured to interact with other students and the teacher, when they would rather just study on their own in the comfort of their home. Virtual can work better for these folks.

It's also harder to establish trust in the virtual space. Unlike the classroom where attendees can see things like body language and where you're moving throughout the room, it's difficult to build the same level of trust in the virtual room. One way to build trust is to really get to know your team members. Spending a few minutes one-on-one with folks helps bridge the gap and build mutual respect so that waiting room or lobby exercise goes a long way to improving your trustworthiness.

Showing up on time (or early), sticking to the agenda, and being prepared also go a long way to enhancing trust. "Walking the walk" and not just "talking the talk" help build a trusting environment.

The virtual room can also create cultural mishaps as we might not be as sensitive to the needs of everyone in the room and end up focusing on those who are engaging with us. In some cultures, it's more common to sit on the sidelines and observe than to get into the lively discussions that can happen. Watch out for any wall flowers in your room and make the effort to get them engaged.

In the classroom, the teacher is at the podium and students choose their seats. This can result in unconscious bias in both the teacher and students about various students' abilities and motivations (front row, back of the hall, etc.), and this can impact learning outcomes.

In the virtual room, the teacher and the students have the same class status and cannot choose one seat over another because the technology assigns your placement on the grid or video feed. The virtual space is easier for instructors to know attendees' names, titles, preferred pronouns, and pronunciation. This enables students to bring their full selves into the open, enhancing their engagement and learning outcomes.

We're still in the early stages of this swing to virtual, so there are still a lot of stereotypes in place regarding the quality of learning a participant receives virtually as opposed to the classroom. This is changing, but the reputation of a virtual degree is still diminished as compared to the traditional academic path.

Once you have determined that a virtual session is the way you want to go, then the heavy lifting begins.

- What are the objectives of your session?
- What are your expected outcomes?
- What are your participant's expected outcomes?

Unlike a full-day event, where you can pack several important lessons into the agenda, virtual sessions are best focused on one or two key items. Any more than that and you're just going to waste everyone's time.

Years ago, when I wrote radio commercials for a living, we used to say that in a thirty-second commercial, you first told the listener you were going to tell them something, then you told them, and then you told them that you told them. There's still a lot of value in that idea, particularly in the virtual room. There is a real need to repeat key content to make sure it sticks. Tell them, tell them again in a different way, and then tell them what you told them. But say it in three different ways—don't just say the same thing over and over. Rephrase and reword to repeat your message.

Don't make the mistake that learners are going to "get it" right out of the gate. Different learning styles require different approaches, so make sure you're repeating the key points in your presentation at least three times, in different ways.

In the virtual space, it's sometimes easier to see if students understand the material. In the classroom, participants often don't answer questions because they don't want to give the wrong answer. In virtual classrooms, you can use things like the polling function to ask the same questions in a multiple-choice format. This can anonymize the responses and increases the number of participants answering the question. You'll soon see if most of them get it or whether you need to circle back on the concept and re-clarify the learning.

Since the students who volunteer to answer questions in class are likely those who understand the material, you can get a false sense that the learning has been understood by everyone. Using tools like polls can help you discover if only half the room understands, and you can clear up the misunderstanding before moving on.

If your objectives for the session are clear, it's far easier to design and deliver a session that meets those objectives. So, getting clear on what learners should take away from your session is a critical first step.

What are the intended outcomes from your session? Are you looking to change behaviour? Introduce a new corporate strategy? Gaining buy-in from stakeholders? Unless you know what learners are expected to take away and act on, it's almost impossible to design a session that delivers.

Chapter 5 – Getting (and keeping) participants involved

Unfortunately, some participants don't want to be in your webinar room.

Sure, some will be eager to learn something new and others are there to brush up on learning or experience something different. But there will be a few who are there because "the manager said I had to attend."

Knowing the reason folks are in attendance in the first place can help you gain—and keep—their attention and participation.

How do you do this?

If you have the opportunity, send out a pre-session questionnaire to registrants. Ask why they're planning to attend. What do they hope to get out of the session? What do they need right now to do their job better? If they could get one thing out of your upcoming session, what would it be? How could they apply it to their job right now? If you can get this kind of input prior to your event, you can bake the answers to their needs and objectives right into the webinar.

As I've already mentioned a couple of times, another good rule to follow is to be sure you open your webinar room at least twenty minutes prior to the session and greet everyone as they arrive. (I normally try to open my webinar room thirty minutes in advance.) As people arrive and join in the session, try to find out a little bit about them. Where are they located? What's their role with the company? Why are they in attendance? In many of the sessions I hosted in the past, there were always one or two "keeners" who showed up very early. In most cases it was to make sure the technology was working, and they were ready to roll at the start time. Other times, they were just excited by the subject and eager to get into the room.

Mark any comments or things you've learned about the person on your attendance list—keep it handy for reference through the session. You can rephrase questions or comments about the material and redirect them to specific participants, like, "Does that sound like something that would help in your role, Sandy?" or "Dean, does that sound like a possible solution to what we were talking about prior to the session?" This helps people focus on the material (they might be called upon to comment) and it helps cement the lesson point to that specific attendee.

Statistically, your room will be filled with folks who are naturally introverted and those who are naturally extroverted. Be sure to appeal to both types. You probably won't have to encourage the extroverts in the room to participate—they're happy to think out loud and offer comments or share stories along the way. But you may have to coax the introverts to speak up or encourage them to use the chat window. Often, introverts take a little longer to process a response as they tend to think before they speak, so allowing them to contribute via the chat window is a good way of getting them to participate without shining a spotlight on them (something they hate).

You can also allow introverts the gift of silence—don't rush into those gaps in the conversation. They may be carefully formulating their answer to your question, and if you jump in too soon, you'll rob them of their contribution to the session.

Now back to those who are in the session because they "have to be there." They may simply be overwhelmed by the experience, being asked to tap into technology they are not familiar with or exhausted by the social demands of the event. They may be awkward with small talk or feel uncomfortable meeting new people or strangers.

Make sure to put these attendees in control of their own experience. Not knowing what to expect, and dealing with uncertainty, these people will become defensive. They won't enjoy the session and they won't get full value from the material as they're constantly evaluating the environment. So put them in control. Make sure every exercise or poll or whiteboard is optional, and don't force them to participate. Focus on delivering real value by making their "pain" worth it. Provide fresh perspectives and deliver an engaging session that provides valuable data that can be of real value to these reluctant guests.

You may have to call on them directly for a comment or ask them to jump on the mic and speak to a question. If you do, remember to refer to your attendance sheet notes to remind yourself of their role or their reason for attending. (If they've told you their reason for attending is because they "have to be there," check to see if they're finding anything of value in what's been said or if any comments by other participants have been valuable or informative).

Helping these attendees connect with the rest of the group and linking the information presented directly to their role or duties in the company can be great ways to increase the value they perceive they're getting from the session. Yet, in the end, no matter how intentional you design your session, there will undoubtedly be the occasional attendee who just doesn't want to be there. Instead of focusing entirely on them, maintain focus on designing and delivering a great experience for everyone there. You're a professional, but you'll never be perfect, so don't get frustrated or angry with them—or yourself.

The basics of virtual.

Here are some of the necessary skills required to successfully deliver a virtual session.

First, you need to understand adult learning principals. This means incorporating the participant's past experiences into the session and using real life examples they can relate to. There's no point in providing an example if it doesn't ring true for them. Chances are your participants have a lot of experience to draw from—the session needs to be designed for all stages of a career, from those just starting out to those who have spent years in the corporate trenches.

Help participants identify their need for the session. And then link the content directly to their day-to-day challenges. It's your first task to "sell" them on the value they'll receive by participating and paying attention during the session. I've found that by telling folks they'll get as much out of a session as they put into it helps set the stage for lively discussions, collaboration, and sharing of ideas.

Appeal to all three learning styles: auditory, visual, and kinesthetic. You're primarily using the auditory and visual channels when you're delivering virtually so you must take the extra steps of incorporating excellent graphics and implementing instructive and interactive exercises throughout the session.

Make sure your slides are bright, clean, and inviting. Speak clearly and change up the pace from time to time to keep auditory learners engaged. Provide interactive windows or chat rooms for those who need to experience lessons on their own. (For PowerPoint tips and tricks, check out Chapter 6.)

If you can, set the stage for your participants with a little pre-work prior to the session. Do you have a pre-recorded overview of what will be covered, and the intended outcomes of the session? Can you provide them with a pre-session worksheet they can use to prepare questions ahead of time, or align the topic to be covered with their unique work issue or challenge? Are there a series of questions or scenarios they might consider in advance so they can prepare to participate to the fullest?

Sometimes, the best advice comes from others in the

same situation, so encourage collaboration and sharing among your participants. I've often seen participants offering up solutions to real-life problems in real-time for fellow attendees. Other times, I've seen participants deciding to connect off-line or post-session to exchange ideas and brainstorm on solutions. Facilitate those exchanges and peer-to-peer learning opportunities, and you'll be the one getting the credit in the end.

Start on time

There will certainly be times when participants are late for your session but forcing those who were on time to sit and wait for the laggards is not very professional. When you're sending out your webinar invitation and link to the virtual room, tell people in advance your session will start on-time. You will be showing respect for those in the room and, just like the physical space, you can deal with the late comers when then arrive.

Starting on time tells your participants you intend to finish on time too, and that is another way of respecting the time commitment each of them is making to attend.

If you do have to backtrack for someone who arrives late, offer to connect one-to-one immediately after the session ends to repeat any information that they might have missed. Reviewing material that the rest of the participants have already gone through isn't very professional and you risk having them disconnect from your session.

Schedule interactions

When you're designing your session, be sure to schedule some sort of interaction with the participants at least every ten minutes. Pull up a poll or a Question module. Engage a white board and get participants to notate or write on it. Get them into breakout rooms for smaller group discussions. Ask them to circle or highlight words on your PowerPoint slide using the drawing tools. Engage them in a task every ten minutes or risk having them tune out, start checking their emails, or disengage entirely and log out of the session.

Schedule breaks

If your session is expected to run longer than ninety minutes, build in some "bio-breaks" for attendees. Let them know in your introduction or your lobby deck that you'll be pausing at X o'clock for ten minutes to let everyone get up and stretch, top up the coffee cup, go to the bathroom, or check their email. This keeps people from wondering when they'll have an opportunity to pop out of the webinar room and helps keep them focused on the material you're presenting.

These scheduled breaks are as important for you as for your participants. Sitting for a couple hours at a time isn't the healthiest idea, so build in some breaks so you too get a chance to stand up, stretch, take a quick walk around your desk or workstation, grab a cup of coffee or a glass of water, and then return to your webinar chair.

Getting up and physically moving will help you reenergize,

so when you do return to the facilitator role, you'll be refreshed and refocused. Again, we're trying to make sure your audience is getting the very best webinar experience possible and you're not going to be delivering that if you're sluggish or uncomfortable. Build in those breaks for selfish reasons.

Some participants may want you to answer a question during the break—try to discourage this. You need the opportunity to move around just as much as everyone else in the webinar room. If you're asked to stay and converse with a single participant, encourage them to hold their question until the group reconvenes or for the Q&A session scheduled for later in the webinar.

And when your break is over, return to the session on time. Let folks know at the start of the break that you'll be starting exactly at X-o'clock. If you've told folks to return in ten minutes, be back in your chair at the nine-minute mark to begin again right on time. This shows respect for your audience and tells everyone you intend to finish on time as well. Your break may be slightly shorter than what your participants get but showing up on time (or ahead of time) is the trait of a real professional.

Don't neglect your audience part way through the session to check your own emails or voice mail. Stay engaged and be a part of the webinar at all times. You'll have time after the session to catch up on emails and calls you may have missed, so don't lose focus during the session. Your audience expects and deserves the best webinar possible.

Chapter 6 – Powering up PowerPoint

One of the biggest mistakes you can make is to use the same slide deck you show in a live session for a virtual delivery. In a face-to-face session, you can leave a slide up on the screen for a couple minutes because the learning is happening in front of it.

You're asking questions, soliciting answers, getting people involved, and speaking. You're moving around the room. People are watching you or concentrating on others in the session who might be speaking. They not forced to stare at the big wall screen displaying your slide.

If you leave a slide up in a virtual session for the same length of time, people will tune you out. Think about your own preferences for a minute. When you're watching something on TV or online, you don't enjoy staring at the same still picture for any length of time. You want visual stimulation—and it's the same with your participants. What might take one slide in a classroom session may take four or five slides in the virtual world. You need to change slides often to keep people focused on their screens. Otherwise, they'll start to multitask, or their attention will drift off to something else more interesting.

Transitions and changes don't need to be big—maybe another sentence is revealed. Or a graphic appears that summarizes what you're talking about. Rather than just letting the slide sit there for any length of time, try livening things up by adding movement, graphics, or transitions. A poorly designed PowerPoint presentation can leave participants confused, bored, or even irritated (and we don't want that). Keep the following key principals in mind.

1. As I mentioned earlier, don't read your presentation from the slides. Your audience can read as well as hear, and they may be able to read things faster than you can speak the words. So don't read verbatim. Paraphrase or re-word what's presented on the screen in the text. This serves two functions. Those visual learners will get the gist of your message as they read what's on the screen, but those auditory learners will benefit from hearing the rephrased message.

Pro Tip

Instead of typing out your entire presentation, include only the main idea, keywords or talking points in your slide show text. Engage participants by sharing the details and deeper content out loud.

2. Follow what PowerPoint calls their "5/5/5" rule. Keep text on a slide to the bare minimum. Some experts recommend no more than five words per line of text, five lines of text per slide, and no more than five text-heavy slides in a row. I'd recommend changing this to a "5/5/3" rule, with no more than three text-based slides in a series. In the virtual space, you'll start losing attention and participation if the scenery gets too text

heavy for any length of time.

Pro Tip

No more than five words per line of text.

No more than file lines of text per slide.

No more than three text-based slides in a row.

When possible, use images instead of text.

For example, don't put up one slide and attempt to talk your way through all the various points: (see below)

This is point one

Point two goes here

Point three goes here

Point four goes here

Above is a bad example of displaying text.

Instead, try breaking up your slide into one requiring transitions after each point is made:

This is point one

First effect in the series.

This is point one

Point two goes here

Click to activate the second point and fade point one.

Advance the slide so the third line appears with points one and two now faded.

Click to reveal the fourth and final line

3. Use readable fonts and colours. Large, simple fonts and theme colours are always a good idea. Since participants are using computer screens, colour settings might be slightly off from one user to another. If you can, stay with recommended themes within PowerPoint to maximize the impact of your text. Also remember light text on dark backgrounds quickly causes eye fatigue.

This is not a good idea. Readers will quickly tire trying to read your slides. Our brains find it easier to read dark text on a light background.

This is a better design. Reading dark text on a light background is easier for your audience. Avoid the use of light text on a dark background.

White text on black vs. regular text.

While dark mode websites seem to be in fashion right now, they are harder to read than regular dark text on a white background. For presentation purposes, keep the audience in mind and don't get distracted by fancy fonts and light text colours.

4. Avoid **ALL CAPS.** They're harder to read and it looks like you're shouting.

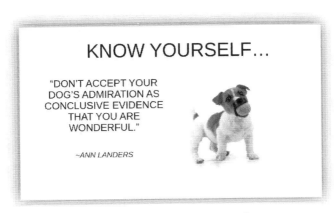

All caps are harder to read.

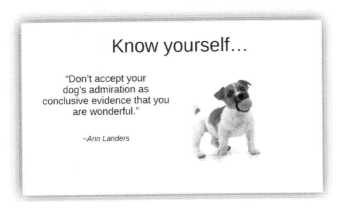

Upper and lower case is what people are used to.

Don't use multiple fonts to add colour or interest. In most cases it only adds to the clutter and confusion users might experience. Keep fonts large and simple (san-serif fonts like Arial or Helvetica are suggested). Serif fonts like Times might have been used in early grade readers, but they don't pack the same punch in the virtual arena. (FYI, Serif fonts have those lines on the ends of letters like this: Liberation Serif.) San serif (French meaning 'without serif') are plainer. This is Liberation Sans, a san serif font.

"Lorem ipsum dolor sit amet, consectetur adipiscing elit, sed do eiusmod tempor incididunt ut labore et dolore magna aliqua."

"Lorem ipsum dolor sit amet, consectetur adipiscing elit, sed do eiusmod tempor incididunt ut labore et dolore magna aliqua".

Serif font on the top; San serif on the bottom.
Which is easier to read?

5. Keep your entire audience in mind. Use humour with caution—not everyone finds the same joke funny, and a clip or goofy effect that might entertain some folks may fall flat with others. While humour can certainly lighten the mood of a presentation, if you're using it inappropriately or in the wrong place, you might be inviting your participants to check out.

Humour also works differently across different age demographics. Your audience may contain a mix of all ages, and some humour that works for one group may not land with others. Keep in mind the total audience before you start relying on humour.

It's important to remember to keep a "smile" in your voice and present from a happy place. It's no fun listening to some Gloomy Gus deliver a session.

6. Don't overuse animations. PowerPoint has some fantastic animation effects. Text and objects can bounce in, fly in from any direct, materialize in bits and pieces, swoop up or down, and so forth. Keep your animations simple, particularly in the virtual arena.

   Don't use every animation that's available—stick to one or two throughout the entire presentation. It helps provide consistency and participants soon learn to watch for them. If you change things up with too many effects, it can seem very unprofessional and disjointed.

   Some platforms don't handle animations very well, and that stunning effect you spent two hours creating suddenly ends up not working. Rehearse your presentation in your chosen platform several times to test transitions and readability of fonts. If you can, log into your platform as a participant, so you can see what your audience will see. If you don't like it, change it. Ask yourself, "Does this part of the presentation need this effect? What does it add to the presentation?" If you're unsure, leave it out.

7. I know I just said not to get too caught up using animations, but they CAN have their place. For instance, having bullet points or bolded text appear as you move through the slide helps focus attention and keeps attendees from reading ahead and disconnecting from the presentation.

   Again, pay attention to the transitions you're using. If you like the idea of the text sliding in from the top or swooping in from the left, stay with that through your presentation. Don't have one set of text slipping in from the left and the next set sliding in from the right—it's hard on the eyes and the brain. And stay away from anything that makes your text shatter or swoop around the slide before landing in place—it's just distracting and looks unprofessional.

8. Make images work for you and your audience. That adage "a picture is worth a thousand words" turns out

to be true. According to Dr. Lynell Burmark, [2] author of Visual Literacy: Learn to See, See to Learn "*...unless our words, concepts, ideas are hooked onto an image, they will go in one ear, sail through the brain, and go out the other ear. Words are processed by our short-term memory where we can only retain about seven bits of information (plus or minus 2) [...]. Images, on the other hand, go directly into long-term memory where they are indelibly etched."*

Both short-term and long-term memory store information in chunks, but short-term memory is limited. One of the easiest ways to ensure that learners store information in their long-term memory is to link concepts to meaningful images. **Images deliver the message faster.**

According to the Visual Teaching Alliance [3]

- The brain can see images that last for just thirteen milliseconds.
- Our eyes can register 36,000 visual messages per hour.

---

[2] Visual Literacy: Learn to See, See to Learn, ISBN-13: 978-0871206404, by **Dr. Lynell Burmark** Published by the Association for Supervision and Curriculum

[3] http://visualteaching.ning.com/

- We can get the sense of a visual scene in less than 1/10 of a second.
- Ninety percent of information transmitted to the brain is visual.
- Images are processed 60,000X faster in the brain than text.
- Forty percent of nerve fibers in the brain are linked to the retina.

All this means is that we human beings process visual information more efficiently than text. See for yourself.

Here's an example of conveying a concept visually, using a graphic, and textually using a text description. We're describing the concept of "What is a square?"

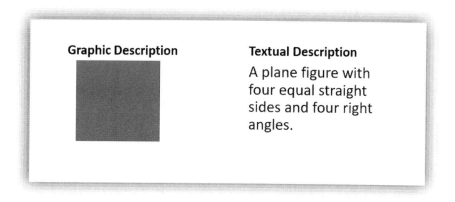

A graphic vs. text

Which works better to describe a square? Which is easier to understand quickly?

What content in your presentation could be better understood as an image or a video, rather than a bullet-list or text box?

Images help trigger emotions, and you are trying to get your attendees attention and focus for your session. What better way than great graphics? Visuals cause a faster and stronger reaction than words. They help users engage with the content and such emotional reactions influence how that information retained. This is because visual memory is stored in the medial temporal lobe of the brain, the same place where emotions are processed. Our brain is set up in such a way that visual stimuli and emotional response is easily linked and together the two form memories. Negative visual depictions are particularly useful for leaving a strong emotional impression. Think of those anti-smoking ads we've all seen with diseased lungs—yuck! Powerful and impactful in getting the message across.

Seeing a picture allows users to recreate the experience in their mind. As a webinar professional you can benefit from this by telling stories in your session through entrancing images and compelling videos.

Caution: it is also important to note that graphics can also negatively impact learning if they are used inappropriately. When off-topic graphics appear on the screen, such as those used for purely decorative purposes, learners will subconsciously try to figure out the message and reason for the image. If they're busy trying to figure something out, then they're not listening – and you've lost them.

The following are types of images to avoid when designing your presentation.

- Pictures that are obviously stock photographs or even worse, clip art.
- Generic graphics that display a clear lack of imagination.
- Poor quality images that are pixelated, low-resolution, over-compressed, or badly resized.

On the other hand, a well-selected image can improve comprehension and insight when you strategically place such graphics within a workshop. Unlike text, pictures have the power to enrich communication and stimulate emotional response. To utilize visuals in a way that will reinforce course material and facilitate learning, it is necessary to use images that:

- Represent actual objects, people, or places.
- Simplify complex or abstract ideas.
- Bridge already learned material and experiences with the unfamiliar or with the new concepts you're presenting.

Only use images that have a clear value, otherwise they are distractions at best and, at worst, give learners the wrong impression. This means omitting anything that does not directly support learning goals.

PowerPoint slides include placeholders for images in the various theme templates. Feel free to experiment with larger images for example. If you've got an image that can tell the story, you really don't need the text field along side it in the template – delete that and expand the image to cover the entire slide, or at the very least most of the slide. You're looking for visual impact here and text can sometimes reduce the punch you might gain with a full screen image.

If you're using an image to tell your story, consider highlighting it in a frame or setting it on a contrasting background. It really is true that a picture is worth a thousand words – so just think of all the text you can avoid with the use of a powerful image.

Pro Tip

When using images, be aware of the file size and the file format of the image you're uploading to your slide deck. Large file sizes can really interfere with the speed of some virtual platforms. Likewise, some file formats don't render or adjust as well as others. I recommend using image files in a .png or .jpg extension. PNG, or portable network graphic files allow you to size up or down without a significant loss in image quality. JPG or JPEG, joint photographic experts group files are usually larger in file size than PNG files and are normally the default file format for things like images created by your digital camera or smart phone.

Pro Tip

Depending on your photo editor there are a couple things to pay attention to when resizing images. When you're opened the image in your photo editor, you can "grab" the corner of the image to resize it – pull it out to make it larger or push it in to downsize the image. Be careful not to squeeze or squash the image. By that, I mean don't reduce the width more than you reduce the height of the image.

Here is an example of what can happen when you resize photos.

Correct.   Squashed.   Stretched.

The left image is properly sized. If I hold down the shift key on the computer (or the control key on my Mac) while dragging a corner "dot", the ratio of height to width will be retained as I enlarge or reduce the size of the image. If I don't hold down the shift key, and simply drag the top of the frame toward the bottom, I end up with the squashed image in the middle. The same holds true if I adjust the width without holding the shift key – I end up with the skinny image on the right.

9. Referring to point #3 earlier, it's always smart to use fonts that are baked into the PowerPoint back end. In PowerPoint themes, there are usually a pair of fonts—one for headings and titles, and another for paragraph test and bullet points. These are matched to provide some consistency across your presentation. However, if you find the standard fonts a little "meh" or have corporate branding that incorporates a different font as a standard, you might want to consider installing your own unique fonts. There are websites like Font Squirrel and DaFont that have thousands of fonts you can download for free, and the web is full of resources to help you pick a font that really works for you. If you decide to go this route, consider Google Font Pairing for more ideas, and to get suggestions for font pairings that work well for you.

10. Consider creating your own colour scheme if you're comfortable using PowerPoint. The program comes with a lot of pre-made colour sets, but perhaps you've got specific corporate colours you'd like to integrate. You can do this by creating custom theme colours, but if you're going this route, again—keep it simple. No more than four or five main colours should be used.

Just because there are twenty-four crayons in a box doesn't mean you have to use them all on every picture. Keeping it clean and tight is the secret to designing a powerful PowerPoint presentation. You'll find links to PowerPoint training online in the Resource section at the end of this book.

Use your slides to reinforce your words, not repeat them.

Chapter 7 – Moving from classroom to web room

What's different – and what's the same?

Much of your session will be just the same as a live event – there will be participants, there will be material to cover and exercises to undertake. There will probably still be the friendly banter among co-workers and maybe even some of the same level of cross-pollination that happens whenever you get a group of people together into a shared space.

And a lot will be different. You won't be sharing the same physical space with folks, so it will be hard to catch those looks of confusion, or the attempt to check that ping on their cell phone. They won't have the same facilitation experience either, so your contagious enthusiasm might not be as easily caught. They'll be staring at a computer monitor if your lucky – they may also be watching on a small tablet or even a cell phone. The technology that makes this all possible is also the technology responsible for making things so difficult at times.

Because there is no common "experience" across attendees, it is up to you as the host and facilitator to constantly check to make sure everyone is following along. Anyone who gets left behind in the session will get less from the workshop, and that's not professional.

The following are a few of the ways you can manage the virtual experience in ways that mimic or mirror the physical workshop.

Icebreakers: setting the stage and getting things underway.

In live sessions, it's not uncommon to take the first few minutes and do a round of introductions – name, department, length of service, maybe a favorite hobby or a word that describes them – you know the drill.

In the virtual space, it's not much different except you might have to orchestrate the introductions a bit more. This is another spot your attendance list can come in useful. Asking folks to jump on the mic and introduce themselves or play along with an icebreaker game is quite easy when you've got a room full of extroverts, but you'll probably want that attendance list to make sure everyone has had a chance to speak. You might want to consider going through the list in alphabetical order, or in following the order of the attendees in the Participant window of your platform. Calling on people gives the introverts a chance to put together a few words in advance when they know they're going to be call on next.

Engage quickly with ice breakers.

What sort of icebreakers can you use that help engage folks from the very start of your session?

If you have the chat window open as attendees arrive, you can get the icebreaker exercise underway immediately. I've often used a short poll asking what the weather is like where the participant is living.

What's the weather like where you are?

- ☐ Sunny
- ☐ Cloudy
- ☐ Rainy
- ☐ Snowy
- ☐ Perfect
- ☐ I've been too busy to look outside

A simple introduction poll.

This is a lighthearted way to get people using some of your webinar program functions at the very beginning of your session (and yes, in Canada, everyone talks about the weather). It also allows me to start of the session with something like "I see about 70% of you are getting sunshine today, so let's make sure we all work together in this session to get the best value from being indoors", or something similar.

Another great idea once the session formally starts is asking people to put their name into the chat window, proceeded by an adjective that starts with the same letter that really describes them. Examples might include:

- Lively Lois,
- Inquisitive Ivan,
- Happy Harpreet,
- Active Alan,

And so forth.

Having people choose their own descriptor goes a long way to get them connected to the content of the session right from the start. They need to think a bit before contributing to the chat, and it's a fun way to see how some folks describe themselves to others.

Different ice breakers may be required when you're working with people from the same team as opposed to a group of random individuals who work for different firms who are attending your session. When you're working with people from the same team, you can use more personalized ice breakers such as the popular "two truths and a lie" exercise. In your pre-work assignment ahead of the session, ask people to come up with three statements about themselves. Two are truths, and the third is a lie. Each person shares with the group their three statements and folks try to identify which is the incorrect statement. The one with the most correct guesses wins. It's a fun and eye-opening exercise when folks learn some of the truths about their fellow team members.

If you can work with an intact team ahead of time, you

might want to encourage them to have a virtual background contest upon entering the room. Ask each participant to upload or select a virtual background for the session and then have everyone vote on who has the best background and why. I've been in sessions where everyone on the team knew each other well so when Kendra showed up with the background of the Mexican Riviera, everyone voted her background the best because she was always talking about going back to Mexico on vacation.

If your session is filled with a group of strangers, then it is up to you to make them feel connected – part of the "group" they're spending time with. One ice breaker I've used over the past eighteen months is asking people what has kept them sane during the lockdowns since nearly everyone has been working from home. I start the exchange, introducing myself and providing a bit of a background on where I'm located in the world and what my role is for the session. Then I'll share a story of how being able to get out into my organic garden has been a safe and satisfying experience over the past many months.

I then pull up a picture of the sign on my garden gate:

The sign hung on my garden gate.

I then open the microphones and ask people to introduce themselves and give a little bit of background on who they are and what they've used to keep themselves level during the pandemic.

I've learned there are a lot of people who have taken up bread making, seriously started exercising again after a lapse, learned to knit, renovated their kitchen, built a gym into their own home, or taken up gardening themselves. These little glimpses into people's personal lives help participants feel like they're part of the group for your session and then they are more likely to stay engaged for the duration.

Peer to peer learning

Often, virtual sessions become a great equalizer across teams. In live sessions, there is still the physical presence of people – particularly managers – who are sitting in on a session and, depending on the business, those people who rank lower on the totem sometimes feel reluctant to speak up and share during live events. Virtual sessions sometimes remove this barrier as people can't see each other, and the hesitancy to speak up is often removed. Try to establish a safe environment for people to speak their mind right from the outset.

If you're having a session with an intact team, it's always advisable to connect with the team lead or manager ahead of time to set the stage for this possibility. You don't want the manager to be "side-swiped" during the session and you want to prepare them for the possibility that people might be less inhibited and say things they might not normally say in a face-to-face session. You can also caution them against responding to comments or keeping some sort of scorecard during the event. Communication across teams is critical and even though there are sometimes things said that we'd rather not hear, it's important for the team to hear them and grapple with the learning and information behind the comment.

Role playing is something that often doesn't work as well in the virtual space as it might in the live training room. I've always cautioned against using role play too much in any session. There are lots of folks – particularly the introverts in the room – who get extremely uncomfortable when put on the spot and asked to "act" something out. They're not going to get much out of a role-playing exercise other than perhaps embarrassment, and the audience isn't going to benefit from their performance either.

In the same way, in the virtual space where you only have your voice to carry the show, it's very difficult to get folks to act out scenarios you might have worked into your live session. Look to see if there are other ways to convey the lesson contained in the exercise. Can it be put into a quiz or poll? Can you use a whiteboard to gather some discussion around the idea and get everyone to contribute rather than asking a couple of attendees to carry the load? Is this a topic that might benefit from sending smaller groups into breakout rooms to discuss and report back?

Many virtual platforms allow you to send people to breakout rooms and those rooms can be equipped with white boards or chat pods that capture the discussions going on there. This makes it easy when attendees are brought back to the general session for someone to recap the discussion within that group and report back to the larger group.

In a F2F session, it's easy for you as a facilitator to check the pulse of the session at any given point. You can see if the material is landing. You can tell if people are disengaging or looking confused. You can read the question someone may have on their face by the puzzled expression, and you can stop at that point and ask for questions.

In the virtual space, you need to stop and check for

understanding several times along the way. There are several reasons for this. In some instances, particularly if you've delivered the material many times in the past, it becomes easy to dance over the learning points because you've heard them over and over before. But that's not the case with your audience, so you need to remember that although YOU may have heard it before, this might all be shiny and new to them, so stop often and check.

Another reason to check is that some attendees may not have English as their first language, so a particular phrase or term you use might not land the same way for them. If you know you've got folks in the audience who fit this description, take the extra time to make sure they're getting the full value of what you're saying.

Most virtual platforms allow you to share material from a variety of sources - your computer desktop, a prepared slide deck via the program app, a pre-recorded video from somewhere like YouTube, and so forth. Become familiar with the program you're using. Test drive it several times using your material to make sure it works, and things like videos play as they should. Nothing derails a presentation quite like having to wait for videos to cue up and play or waiting for files to download before you can use them.

Set things up in advance so you're not cutting into your presentation time with interruptions. It doesn't look very professional when you need to wrestle with the technology part-way through your presentation. Prepare in advance, rehearse, and practice, practice, practice.

Every professional will tell you practice makes perfect.

Chapter 8 - Tales from the trenches and lessons learned

Here are a few stories of things that have happened in the world of webinars over the past couple years, along with what lessons were learned along the way.

Logistics

In April of 2020 a company had planned to send fourteen senior executives to a leadership development workshop, but the office was suddenly locked down due to the Covid-19 pandemic and the trainer was not permitted to enter the building. The event was altered to move into a virtual space to allow the facilitator to continue to present on the original date.

Unfortunately, on the day of the workshop, all fourteen gathered in the company boardroom around a single Jabra telephone connection and a computer projected onto one of the screens in the room. Having all the participants gathered around a single computer prevented the facilitator from successfully using the chat window, the polling option, and the whiteboard which she'd worked into the session. Individual speakers had to lean into the telephone speaker to be heard. None of the attendees were able to be seen via the webcam, and the facilitator had to scrap the breakout sessions she had planned and instead wound up conducting a larger group dialogue around the leadership issues she was attempting to facilitate. As a result, the session was much less impactful than it was designed to be.

Lessons learned:

Following the event, the facilitator worked with the session sponsor to develop a new set of invitations and instructions to be sent out prior to virtual sessions. Participants were instructed to log into the event from their own computer or workstation and to have their own microphone and speakers to access the audio channel. Instructions included a list of expectations for each of the participants which included them contributing to the chat, answering some questions, working with the polling module, and collaborating using whiteboards in breakout rooms. Setting these expectations in advance made subsequent sessions run more smoothly and increased interaction and participation.

Take away:

Let participants know your expectations for the session well in advance, including things like having individual computer access to the event and their own audio connection.

Power failure

In early 2021, we had a session planned for nine individuals who had missed an in-house training session and needed to catch-up on the material that was presented earlier to the rest of their team. Moments before the scheduled start time, we lost electrical power (a traffic accident knocked out a transformer and killed the power to a wide area). This was after many of the participants had logged into the system and we were waiting for the session to start.

Since we had the individual email addresses of all the attendees, I was able to contact each of them using my laptop and my wireless hotspot from my phone to update them on the situation and suggest that once we were up and running again, we would reschedule the event. We were able to connect with all the participants within about three minutes and were able to shift the session to another date.

Lessons learned:

Be prepared for technical interruptions by having access to your webinar via another device where you can contact attendees with an update. This wasn't the first time we've had power disruptions and, as a result, I've baked in some of the fall-back plans like having a hotspot connection and making sure my laptop was fully charged before the session. I also log into the session as a participant with my laptop, which can be quickly reconnected to the session via my hot spot if my regular internet connection becomes unavailable.

Take away:

Be sure to have a "Plan B" for every event you have planned. You may not ever need it, but if something happens, you'll be able to quickly connect back with attendees and update them on any changes.

Late admissions

About a year ago, I held a session for a group of team members who had missed a training event. I'd worked with the team lead on getting things in place and, with less than twenty-four hours before the scheduled start time, I got an email from them asking if they could add one more person to the session. There was pre-work involved for the session, which included watching two pre-recorded videos and answering a short questionnaire based on the content. I was told this new addition would complete the pre-work.

On the day of the session, it soon became very clear this person hadn't bothered to watch any of the videos and had no comment on any of the questions I'd posed around the material. They continually interrupted with questions that would have been unnecessary if they'd done what they said they would do, and these interruptions forced me to stop and try to get this person up to speed with the material as we progressed. Based on the facial expressions of some in the webinar room during my answers to these questions, it was obvious they were not impressed with their teammate, and they were losing interest and engagement in the session.

Lessons learned:

Last-minute registrants should only be considered if you know they won't derail your presentation. If you have pre-work for them to complete, don't accept any late attendees if there isn't enough time for them to complete it.

Take away:

Set up a reasonable "late admissions" schedule for your session, particularly if it involves any pre-work or having people prepare items for submission or discussion. Then, be prepared to stick to that timeline. Holding up any session to answer questions that were answered in pre-work can derail engagement very quickly. And once your attendees are disengaged, it's very difficult to get the momentum going again and keep the pace.

No introduction

One person told me about a session they attended where the facilitator just jumped right into the material without any introduction or preparation. The instructor saw the number of people on the attendee list matched the number they were told would be in attendance and launched into their slide deck. This caught almost everyone off-guard, and there were lots of interruptions by attendees during the first several minutes wanting to know how to open the chat window and others who had no idea whether they could be heard on the audio stream. It made for a very rocky start. The facilitator had to stop and back up many times to make sure attendees could participate in the session.

Lessons learned:

It's always necessary to take a moment or two at the very

beginning of a webinar to introduce (or re-introduce) features and tools you'll be using throughout. Instead of assuming everyone will know where to find things, and how to use them, always set the stage for attendees so they get maximum benefit from your webinar without feeling left behind.

Take away:

Don't overlook the importance of a lobby deck or welcome area for your event. You'll avoid a bunch of questions later in your session when you set your attendees up for success in advance.

Repurposed slides

Someone who had attended a team building experience online told me they were not impressed. The facilitator for the event was an in-house human resources trainer who had facilitated this type of team session many times in the past. They tried to use their regular deck of PowerPoint slides and met with several problems. Three short videos embedded into slides did not play on the webinar software being used. Several slides had so many lines of type that were difficult to read on the smaller computer screens as they were designed to be projected on a large in-house screen. There were also a couple team building exercises that did not translate into the virtual space, so they were skipped by the facilitator who then sat and explained what the exercises were and what their intended outcome was supposed to be.

<u>Lessons learned:</u>

Taking your regular slide deck and using it online without thinking about how planned exercises need to be "translated" into the virtual space is a recipe for disaster. Having people stand around a flip chart in a live session is a lot different from when they're trying the same exercise from their own computer.

<u>Take away:</u>

Make sure any exercises have been translated into the virtual arena, and don't load slides with long sentences or text that just never ends. Refer to Chapter 6 for additional PowerPoint tips and suggestions.

No follow up

I was told by another attendee a virtual session they attended did not have anything in the way of follow-up survey or response form. They were disappointed because they had a couple problems during the session and wanted the facilitator to know they should be addressed so any additional sessions wouldn't have the same problems.

<u>Lessons learned:</u>

Response forms and follow-up evaluations are extremely important for improving future sessions. Don't think of them as a criticism of the session but as a way to continually improve your presentations.

<u>Take away:</u>

Design a simple and effective evaluation survey you can send attendees following every session. You may not get a lot of responses, but the information contained in the ones you do receive can be very helpful in planning and delivering future webinars.

No relevant examples

I've had several attendees tell me about sessions they've attended over the past year-and-a-half where the examples used by the facilitator didn't seem to apply to their working situation. One told me about attending a course designed for senior level accounting managers in the health services sector where the spreadsheet examples were all based on a freight hauling business. This person found it hard to translate the example data into their real-world experience. They spent a lot of time trying to apply the knowledge.

<u>Lessons learned:</u>

Design your session examples in such a way they can be easily understood by those in attendance.

<u>Take away:</u>

Make sure any examples you include in your session are relevant to the attendees. Check back through Chapter 3 for the section under Relevant.

Chapter 9 – Facilitate, don't teach

Facilitate comes from the French word "facile," which means "easy." When you facilitate, you're trying to make it easy for people to learn.

Teaching is often defined as a process where a teacher leads a group of students in attaining new abilities, knowledge, or skills. It's an intensive process of sharing knowledge with the aim of increasing psychological and intellectual growth of an individual. It's often considered a "one-way" or "top-down" process of learning transfer.

Facilitating is the act of engaging participants in creating, discovering, and applying learning or concepts. Facilitation is a two-way stream of learning in that the instructor and students are co-creating the learning experience.

Let's stack the two side by side and compare the differences between Teaching and Facilitating.

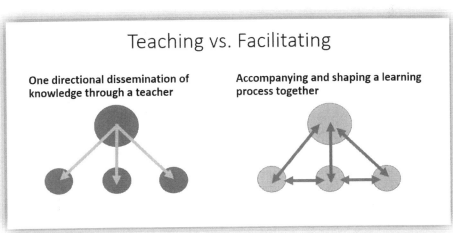

Teaching vs. Facilitating.

Teaching	Facilitating
Content is teacher-centered; delivery is designed to meet curriculum standards	More student focused with delivery dedicated to learning
Known as "*sage on the stage*" where the teacher delivers the content to the audience and is more focused on their content than the needs of participants	More of a "*guide on the side*" who engages participants in different activities, asks questions, encourages participation, and moderates discussions
Teacher seen as the subject matter and the delivery matter expert	The facilitator is the learning process expert who guides the participants through the material
Teaching is mainly focused on learning via instruction and a set of exams or quizzes to measure content retention	Facilitation assists participants to learn together as a group, or to accomplish together as a group
The way of learning is decided by the teacher	In facilitation, learners and facilitators coordinate the session together
This style of learning involves reading, listening, and remembering	More collaborative and involves recognizing, reflection, and application of the content
The teacher is accountable for how much information the student learns	The facilitator helps to estimate what group members learned from their session
While "teaching" covers a wide variety of delivery methods, the one most associated is the term "lecture style"	Facilitating is a delivery method where the facilitator circles the material and helps participants to direct it

Teaching	Facilitating
The main priority is concepts and theories	The priority is on experience and then connecting those experiences to subject material
Traditionally a one-way interaction, teacher to student. Less interaction	Two-way interaction in facilitation allows everyone in the group to express their opinion and feel like a major part of the group, serving their best to the group
More appropriate for children, i.e., school classes	More appropriate for adults and virtual delivery
Participants expected to be obedient students, clients, or employees	Participants encouraged to participate and challenged to apply concepts to real world situations immediately
In most cases topics are recommended by the teacher	Inspires participants to follow thought-provoking and appropriate topics
Teacher helps to add new knowledge	Helps to connect new knowledge with past experiences and current needs
More acceptable in art, music literature, and academia	Designed to build a community and world that is suitable in participants global views and perception
Students held responsible for being on exact timetable, routine, and complete work on time	Each person is answerable to the group and for themselves

As I've said a couple times, say it—don't read it. I can't stress this enough. Don't fall into the easy trap of reading the text on your slides. It's better to paraphrase the contents. You're working with adult learners who can read just fine. Nothing is more irritating than listening to someone reading text you've already read and understood.

Instead of typing your entire text on the slide, reduce the sentence down to one or two key words or phrases. You don't have to have complete sentences—in fact it's better if you don't. Here's an example:

- The last quarter's financials were stronger than projected.

- Quarterly results surprising

Which point might generate more interest?

Rather than having something like that top bullet point, which everyone can read and requires very little explanation, try something like the second bullet point.

The second shortened version helps to engage the viewer as it doesn't tell the entire story. What is the surprise in the quarterly results? Is it a good surprise or one not so good? Which one do you think will grab the attention of participants?

You don't need to worry about punctuation too much if you're reducing your text to bullet phrases and key words. Unlike this book, where sentence structure and punctuation are necessary to the overall story, PowerPoint slides don't have to be works of literary art. Keep the attendees in mind. Can you convey the concept with an image or picture? There are lots of internet sites and providers who can provide the perfect image to capture what you're trying to say. Lots of these are even free, but a subscription to a good image bank can be worth the investment if you're serious about adding visual power to your presentations.

I've included links to a half-dozen image bank websites in the Resources section at the end of this book but there are scores more.

Make the learning easy.

Why fluff up your message with a five-dollar word when a ten-cent word will say the same thing and not be off-putting to attendees. For example, instead of saying something like "at the present time" try "now". Instead of saying "close proximity" try "nearby".

Pro Tip

For more information on using simple words and phrases, as well as recommendations for word substitution, check out

https://www.plainlanguage.gov/guidelines/words/use-simple-words-phrases/ an official website of the United States Government.

Chapter 10 – Check for understanding; learning transfer

Your webinar is the vehicle you're using to convey some information or learning, but it's not the product. Simply by attending your session there's no guarantee the participant will take away anything of value from the session – unless you're purposeful in design, delivery, and deployment.

It's that last one – deployment, or implementation – that sometimes goes off the rails. You can spend hours getting the design perfected and polish the delivery until you know it backwards and forwards. And all that means nothing if the subject matter doesn't land because it can't be used. Unless the content is relevant and relatable to the participant, it's just another web session.

Many of us remember our school and university years. The teacher delivered a lesson and we students made notes, memorized, set up flash cards, attended study groups... whatever it took to regurgitate the material to a level that merited a passing mark. Rinse and repeat. In the virtual world, the facilitator is not the teacher, but more of a guide or navigator for attendees. It's our job to highlight the lesson, sure, but it's even more important we're able to put that lesson into a context that matters for the participant. Unless they can quickly apply the learning, they have no more than they had six months after that high school chemistry final – not much.

When I was growing up, I was a member of a 4-H club. 4-H has been around more than a hundred years and is a highly respected positive youth development organization. 4 H clubs are found in more than 70 countries and believe in nurturing responsible, caring and contributing leaders who are committed to positively impact their communities (you can check them out at https://www.4-H.org.)

The motto of 4-H is "Learn to Do by Doing". There's real power in applying the learning straight out of your session, but you can magnify this effect by getting participants to use the learning while they are still **in** the virtual space.

Ask them for real life examples of where your lesson can be applied in their workplace or life right now. Let them play with the ideas and concepts and apply them in their world while they're in the session. If they're unable to do that, then ask for a timeline when they will be able to put the learning to use – it helps anchor the importance of your lesson and greatly improves the chances they'll act quickly to get maximum impact from your session as they have chosen an application or implantation date

Is there a quiz or poll you can create that translates your lesson material into real-world situations for your learners? Can you get them to connect the dots between what your session is about to actual situations in their workplace? Making your webinar relatable helps make the material you're providing actionable. And this helps the material stick.

Improve learning transfer

Learning transfer is defined as the ability of a learner to successfully apply the knowledge, skills and behaviour acquired in a learning event to their job, with a resulting improvement in their performance. While your session might get top-marks and great feedback, if people can't apply what they learn to their job, the training has missed its mark. Wikipedia defines Transfer of Learning as what occurs when people "apply information, strategies, and skills they have learned **to a new situation or context."**

Thinking back to the "M" in the "ARM and a LEG" principles, when a new piece of information enters our working memory, we search our long-term memory for any association which combine with the new information in working memory. This association reinforces the new information and helps assign meaning. Learning that takes place in varying contexts can create more links and encourage generalization of the knowledge or skill.

Connections between past learning and the new learning can provide a context or framework for the new information, and that helps learners determine sense and meaning, and encourages retention of the new information. These connections then build up a framework of associative networks that the learner can call upon for future problem solving.

Factors that may affect the transfer of learning from your session include the following:

- The context and amount of original learning: how well has the learner acquired the knowledge?
- Similarity: what are the common links between their original learning and the new, such as environment and other memory cues?
- Critical attributes: what are the characteristics that make the content unique?
- Association: what are the connections between this event, action, or bit of information with the person's past experiences? What conditions and emotions are connected to the new material by the learner?

Learners can increase their ability to apply this new material through effective practice and by mindfully abstracting knowledge. Abstraction is a process of examining our experiences for similarities. This might include seeking the underlying principles in what is learned, creating models, and identifying analogies and metaphors, all of which assist with creating associations and encouraging transfer. As webinar professionals we need to assist our participants to make their own direct links between the new material and their own past experiences and knowledge.

Very often, it's not the training that's the problem. It's what comes afterward. The biggest challenge for most organizations is what happens **after** the webinar. Most companies still see training as a singular event rather than an on-going process. Once the training session is over, companies want employees back on the job, not investing even more precious company time in team practices and evaluation sessions with peers and supervisors.

Putting staff back into additional training rooms is expensive, so many companies create job aids to help reinforce the learning and hope that's enough to anchor the learning.

In 2006 Will Thalheimer wrote, "Spacing Learning Events Over Time: What the Research Says." [4] Thalheimer stated that while learning and memory may be strong during a training event, knowledge is rapidly forgotten afterwards. He illustrated this concept with the following 'Learning and Forgetting Curves' which outline the need for on-going on-the-job reinforcements after any learning event.

---

[4] https://www.worklearning.com/wp-content/uploads/2017/10/Spacing_Learning_Over_Time__March2009v1_.pdf

Typical Learning and Forgetting Curves

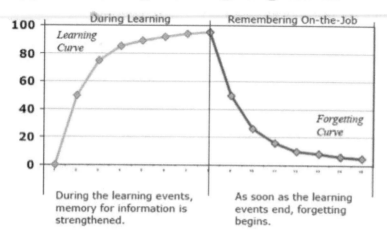

Learning and Forgetting Curve.

SOURCE: Thalheimer, W. (2006, February). "Spacing Learning Events Over Time: What the Research Says," retrieved August 19, 2021, from http://www.work-learning.com/catalog

He also observed that spaced repetition or reinforcements on the job **after** training influenced how much people will remember and apply to their work. He also suggested that *"the closer in time learning is delivered to the situations when it is needed, the less forgetting will be a factor. The less forgetting, the more learners will be able to remember what they learned and apply it to their jobs."*

Learning and Forgetting with Spacing On-the-Job

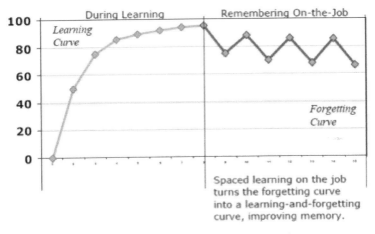

Learning with Follow-up Sessions.

SOURCE: Thalheimer, W. (2006, February). "Spacing Learning Events Over Time: What the Research Says," retrieved August 19, 2021, from http://www.work-learning.com/catalog

The virtual space is the perfect arena for applying these spaced repetitions Thalheimer recommended. The webinar room is a perfect place to start chunking-up the material into more bite-sized pieces. Instead of trying to cram everything into one single session that may be quickly forgotten, virtual allows you the opportunity to create multiple mini sessions that can assist employees to embed the learning over an extended period. As an example, a couple ninety-minute learning bursts coupled with breaks of an hour or more can set the learner up for greater retention of the material than plowing along for two or three hours at a time.

You may want to consider reinforcing your webinar with post-session job aids, or a weekly email that helps amplify the material in your webinar and increases the relevance of your material to the participants' jobs. Work with your client or sponsor to develop this post-session reinforcement. If you're the "in-house" facilitator for your organization, develop a plan to follow up on the virtual session you host with bite-sized reinforcements.

This type of post-session support only takes a few minutes of time, so it minimizes the impact on the employee's job. It can greatly enhance retention of the materials covered in your webinar and increase the long-term effectiveness of the training. It also puts the responsibility and control of the learning into the hands of the participant, and it can remove the need for ongoing training from the employee's supervisors or peers.

More ideas for in-house facilitators

Reflection is one of the best ways to anchor the knowledge, identify gaps in training, and identify any barriers to a strong knowledge transfer. I recommend sending follow-up emails to attendees immediately following the session. You can even include a homework assignment for them to apply what they just learned. Reinforce key learning points with a virtual exercise a week or two later, drawing on the material you've presented, and then arrange additional follow-up sessions as needed to provide supplemental lessons. You can also use these opportunities to allow trainees to apply their knowledge on the job to practice their skills or discuss their experiences by giving them a specific mock project on work on.

Online learners are more likely to engage when they know their opinions are valuable to you. Therefore, ask your attendees for ongoing e-learning feedback. Conduct surveys and social media polls to get their input or invite them to participate in focus groups for an upcoming e-learning course. This allows you to incorporate their suggestions and observations to improve your e-learning strategy and ensure that your content is still on target.

Creating a monthly newsletter your online learners can opt-in to can be a final call to action in your training presentation. So long as it links back to their learning objectives at the outset of the session, you might focus on a new discussion topic in each edition, including useful tips and tricks. The key is to inspire online learners and provide them with real value. You can even invite subject matter experts to write guest posts and provide their unique perspective.

If you have the resources, create an e-learning podcast or video series that describes a new topic each month. You can upload podcasts directly to your e-learning course site or platform. There are also several video sharing sites that can help you reach your target audience. These online resources can even allow you to attract new online learners and keep them in the loop. For best results, set a schedule in advance so that online learners know when to tune in.

It's also critically important to remember you really can't teach something to someone – they need to want to learn it. It's not as simple as opening a mind, pouring in some learning, and sealing up the container again. Knowledge transfer is only effective when it's applicable. That means instead of keeping that old teaching model where the instructor is the "keeper of the keys," what about thinking of the participant as the knowledge keeper? You're there to help them add to their arsenal or tool kit, not to provide a whole new tool. Think of what you're providing as an additional attachment to their "Swiss army knife" of knowledge; you're upskilling what they already use.

By keeping the participant at the centre of the event from the very first planning phase, you set them up to succeed in gaining and retaining the information you're presenting by giving them an **"ARM and a LEG."**

Applicable
Can your participants use the learning right away?

Relevant
Are you using real life examples?

Memorable
How 'sticky' is your session?

Lean
Have you eliminated all the fluff and filler?

Engaging
How are you going to connect and hold onto participants?

Genuine
Are you enjoying it or faking it?

ARM & LEG detailed.

Keeping the above listed principles in mind when you're putting together your webinar and for any subsequent follow up will help your participants get maximum value from your session.

Chapter 11 – The trouble with technology

The common denominator across all webinars and virtual training sessions is technology and there are a lot of moving parts in that word.

There's the webinar software you've chosen to use. The webcam you're using. The audio feed for your session. The computer system you're operating. The computer system your participants are using. Some folks will be attending from their home computer; others will be joining from a company workstation, and that can make for a very un-levelled playing field. Some are tech-savvy and others are not.

So, it's not a question of **if** something is going to go wrong, but **WHEN** it will go wrong.

How can you anticipate, prepare for, and recover from technology trouble when it arrives?

Let's take it in pieces, looking at the various things that can go wrong.

Your webinar software

A webinar is nothing more than the combination of the word "web" and "seminar." Webinar software is the stuff behind the scenes that run the online presentation. You can call it a meeting or event or a live presentation via the internet, but in the end, you're going to need a robust and reliable webinar software program to deliver a professional session.

Your choice of which webinar software you're going to use can have an influence on the end-user experience. There are dozens of programs and platforms out there from which to choose – and they all have benefits and drawbacks. They range in price from free to very expensive, and it is a good idea to thoroughly investigate the program you consider using to make sure it offers a good balance of features for you and benefits for your attendees.

A simple Google search will turn up dozens of sites offering things like *"The 10 best webinar software platforms of 2021"* or *"21 Best Webinar Software of 2021"*. These can be a good start to begin exploring options that might work for you. There is a note of caution however: some of these sites have affiliate connections with the software program they're recommending. This means the author of the site may receive a commission or fee from software purchases that are redirected from that site, so a particular software recommendation may not be completely unbiased.

I've listed four of the industry leaders in the reference section at the back of this book. They are webinar programs that have proven themselves year over year, long before Covid-19 sent thousands of facilitators scrambling onto the web. The four programs I've listed include:

- Adobe Connect
- Cisco WebEx
- Google Hangouts

- Zoom

Again, there are dozens of other programs available so do your research and find the tool that fits your budget AND your needs. Check out user reviews and pay particular attention to things like audio quality and participant limits. Ease of use may be important to you, but even more important is how easy the program is to use by your attendees.

Some questions to consider when looking for a webinar software program include:

Lobby or waiting room

Think of this as the gathering space before your actual webinar starts. What is the lobby or waiting room experience like for your participants? Can you have lobby music, or a count-down timer? Can you have a live feed of your web camera playing in the corner so attendees will see their host as they sign in? Can you run a check-in poll or quiz or open the Chat window to get people connecting and collaborating even before the actual session begins?

You don't want the experience to be like visiting the doctor's office where all the magazines are over a year old. Even your lobby experience should be inviting, engaging, and entertaining.

User experience

Does the program you choose require participants to download a plugin or app to join the meeting? If so, are they able to do this? Many corporate IT departments prevent employees from installing new programs on their workstations, so investigate in advance. How compatible is the program to various devices – desktops, laptops, tablets, mobile phones?

Host limits

Does your software choice allow multiple presenters? Can you share the floor with another presenter for a tag-team session? Is it a program you can run on your own as a host and presenter if necessary, or do you require an additional set of hands and eyes to operate the Host function while you present?

There may be times when you want to have a co-presenter or guest speaker. Make sure your choice of platforms allows you that option. It doesn't look very professional when you must sign out so your guest presenter can sign in.

Audio

This is probably one of the most important considerations because any interruption or drop in sound quality is a major disruption for your viewers. Participants may forgive some inferior video quality, but if the sound is off or there are audio problems that prevent them from hearing your session, they'll turn you off. Check the user reviews for the webinar software you're considering, paying particular attention to any comments about insufficient or poor audio quality.

It may also make a difference on the type of microphone you're using for your webinar. Are you using a stand-alone microphone, or something like a boom mic? Are you using the ear buds and microphone from your phone? Headphones? The microphone built into your webcam? Each of these audio input devices can sound different to your audience. For example, if you're using the mic built into your computer, it can sound like you're speaking from the bottom of a barrel or in an echo chamber. Headsets can allow you to adjust the microphone too close to your mouth and you end up sounding like you're shouting, or your voice is amplified and distorted. You are also at risk of the mic picking up your breathing sounds if the mic is too close to your mouth or nostrils.

Also make sure you're not picking up background noises during your session. No one wants to hear the dog barking next door or be distracted by noises off stage.

Capacity

What's the webinar room capacity? While many of your sessions may be smaller in terms of attendees, if you're looking to host a session for a hundred or more participants, you'll need to be sure your software is able to accommodate that number. In most cases, the larger the room capacity, the higher the price you'll pay for the software. Some programs offer a "bump-up" option that allows you to expand a room for a one-time event - usually for a one-time additional fee but check to be sure. You may never need this feature but it's nice to have in the event you do wind up hosting something that's bigger than your regular session.

Backgrounds

What's behind you when you're online? Is your background neat or a distraction?

Is your audience trying to decipher the meaning of the abstract painting on the wall behind you or are they counting the figurine collection you've so lovingly assembled?

Does the program allow you to blur your background or show a virtual background instead of what's really in the background behind you? If you're like a lot of presenters who don't have a "studio set-up" to host your sessions from, you may be operating from a home or office workspace that has some clutter behind you. Having a program that allows you to blur or hide the background can be helpful. You don't want participants distracted by things they can see just over your shoulder. I've heard of sessions where participants were trying to read the titles of books on the shelf behind the presenter – certainly a sign they weren't engaged in the subject matter.

Try to create an inviting appearance by being intentional about your background setup. Take the time to make sure you're putting your most professional face forward every time you deliver a session.

One note of caution: Some virtual backgrounds create a "halo" effect around you as it blurs the background. This can create a cut-out effect that distorts your image where it overlaps your actual backdrop. When you move, you generate a pixilated effect that can be distracting and annoying to watch for extended periods of time. Test your software to ensure it doesn't create this distortion effect.

Again, log into your platform as a participant to see for yourself what your audience will see. If you don't think it is professional enough, then change it.

Webcams

Nearly all laptops come with built-in cameras and microphones, and if you're using a laptop to host your session, practice in advance with the webcam feature. Depending on the placement of the laptop, your webcam might be showing viewers a less-than-flattering view of you: no one wants to be staring up the presenter's nose for two hours. You also don't want to appear to be looking down on your audience.

Where are you sitting relative to your background and the frame of your webcam? Do you want people to see you from the waist up or just your head? These decisions can impact how easily participants find they can connect with you. I like to be just a little off-centre in the screen, so I've got room for hand gestures or to hold up props when necessary.

Remember to sit up straight with your feet flat on the floor. If you're slouching, how serious will someone take you?

Continue to use body-language in the virtual space. While

you're limited from moving around too much you still can vary facial expressions, gesture, lean into important parts of your presentation and lean away to invite group chats and peer-to-peer exchanges. People sometimes forget to use body language when seated and there's nothing worse than watching a talking head for ninety minutes who is clearly reading a prepared script in a dull monotone while impersonating a statue.

Many professional actors trained for the stage find it hard to transition to television. They're trained to exaggerate gestures on stage so the folks in the back row can get the act, but television requires a much more subtle approach. Raising an eyebrow on stage might be seen by the folks up front, but on television, even a slight twitch in the corner of your eye can be zoomed in on for a powerful effect. So, if you've trained to present live and-in-person, you may want to consider some of the actions or movements you worked into your routine and be more reserved – more subtle and less physical – in the virtual space.

Look at the camera – not the audience. If you're fortunate enough to be able to have a host or second presenter for your session, you can concentrate on watching the webcam instead of also having to keep an eye on the chat window, raised hand status, attendees' video grid and more. Direct eye contact is what you're going for here. It can be a challenge to focus on your camera during a session – especially when others are speaking – but you will increase the impact of your session when you look deep into that dot on the webcam. It will probably feel uncomfortable, but politicians and entertainers have been doing this for years.

If you must fly solo on your presentation and keep an eye on all the pods, polls, chats and so forth, return to the webcam every chance you get. It's no different than shifting focus in a live session where one minute you may be looking Guldeep in the eye as she asks a question and the next connecting eye-to-eye with Alan as he makes a point. As participants, we're used to having people look elsewhere so don't make the mistake of staring at the webcam without any glances away. That can begin to feel uncomfortable – like someone is staring at you– so try to remember to break eye contact from time to time.

If you wear glasses, consider what might be reflected in the lenses back to your viewers. If you don't want to invest in a laptop stand to raise your computer and give the camera a more "straight on" view, prop your laptop up on a couple textbooks or an empty box. That will also help prevent your viewers from seeing your ceiling, any additional lighting you're using for your session, or the fancy woodwork around your cabinets instead of focusing on you.

Finally, don't become your own distraction. Yes, your video feed is up there in the grid with everyone else, but don't get distracted on how flat your hair looks today or your choice of jacket colour for the session. If you've prepared in advance, try to relax, and remember that if this were a live session, you wouldn't be able to view yourself on the monitor anyway, so why start now? If you're concentrating on you, you're not connecting with your participants.

Lighting

You don't need to be set up like a television studio but lighting really does make a difference.

If your space is filled with natural light, fantastic. Just remember to make sure it's in front of you, and not coming from behind because that puts you into a shadow, and your webcam will be overpowered by the light coming in over your shoulder.

If there are shadows on your face, you might want to consider additional lighting such as desk lamps, or even webcam lights (sometimes called halo lights or ring lights) that surround the lens of your webcam. This helps fill in the lighting on your face and eliminates those pesky shadows. Harsh shadows on your face can make the overall atmosphere feel dark and uninviting. Just make sure any additional lighting isn't causing harsh reflections in your glasses (if you wear them).

If your room is too bright, invest in some curtains but don't darken things so much you create shadows on your face.

You want your appearance to be inviting so you don't detract from your presentation.

Breakout rooms

Breakout rooms are ideal for smaller discussions and really contribute to peer-to-peer learning and exchanges. But all breakout rooms are not created equally and depending on the webinar software you choose breakout rooms can have you curled up on the floor in a fetal position weeping to yourself in no time at all.

Some of the problems with breakout rooms include:

- the audio channel not following the participant into the breakout room,
- some attendees are not able to join a breakout room,
- an attendee gets "kicked out" of a breakout room for some unknown reason,
- some breakout rooms require the attendee to "click to join." (If that's the case with your program, let participants know in advance or they may wind up spending a lot of time trying to figure out why they're not automatically moved to a breakout room.)

Do a Google search for "problems with breakout rooms" to pull up a laundry list of various issues associated with a wide range of webinar software. It might help you narrow down your choice of webinar software.

In some cases, breakout rooms don't work because attendees aren't joining from a computer. I've had participants logging into a session while on vacation, and they're using the iPad they packed along or even their cell phone. While I did appreciate they were taking time from their holiday to be a part of the session, the technology they were using created problems for themselves and everyone else in attendance. Many webinar software programs are not designed for mobile devices. Make sure your webinar invitations spell out any potential equipment requirements or limitations in advance. Don't assume your attendees will know what correct technology to use for your session.

In some instances, the internet connection the participant is using might be causing the problem. In other cases, it might be the web browser they've chosen – and a lot of people are using browsers that aren't kept up to date with updates and patches. Some organizations control the computers employees work from, and not all IT departments are equal when it comes time to rolling out user updates or keeping things patched.

The caution here is breakout rooms should be used sparingly – and only if you're reasonably certain the program you're using has a robust breakout room feature.

If you do choose to use breakout rooms, try to pre-populate or pre-assign these in advance if possible. Consider assigning people to certain rooms in advance. Some programs allow you to set this up ahead of the session. Otherwise, unless you're using a Host in your session, you'll be forced to multi-task getting the attendees sent off to various rooms while maintaining the tempo of the webinar.

Most breakout rooms allow you to send chat messages into each room so you can send updates or instructions. You can post the question you've asked them to discuss. You can alert them that the breakout session will be ending in two-minutes to allow them time to wrap up any conversations or capture the final notes to present back to the larger group.

Remember: if you use breakout rooms, be sure to provide some discussion time for attendees once they return to the whole group again. The conversations that can occur in breakout rooms can be rich in content so make sure groups have a chance to present back to the larger assembly once they're returned. If you've asked them to whiteboard ideas in their breakout rooms, make sure you've built in enough time to allow each room to present back to the broader audience.

Pro Tip

Get a half-dozen friends, family, or co-workers together and rehearse the breakout function in your chosen webinar software. Play with it. Practice and look for flaws or problems. You probably won't be able to predict every error or issue, but you'll be better prepared than if you have no experience and suddenly have issues you can't resolve. Having a breakout session go off the rails does not make you look very professional.

White boards and notation functions

Almost all webinar software programs allow for notations and text functions from participants. These are helpful in many ways but particularly from the standpoint of keeping people engaged in the presentation.

Putting up a slide and asking people to circle certain words, or underline things or to put check marks or XX's on statements gets people involved and helps generate a visual that demands attention. People like to see where their comment or line is placed relative to others in the session.

Drawing tools

Drawing tools allow users to select a virtual pencil or marker, choose an ink colour, and works like the white board notation tool. Again, the idea is to get people interacting and keep them engaged in the session. Asking them to colourize a drawing or personalize an ink colour gives them a unique reason and opportunity to keep engaged in the session.

This can also be helpful as a facilitator. You can call out participants based on what you're seeing happening on the screen. "Someone using the broad tip red marker is highlighting a lot of issues here. Could I ask you to please jump on the mic and elaborate a little further?"

Regardless of the webinar software you choose, dig into the back end, and become familiar with all the tools in the toolbox. Your participants will thank you, and your session will run much more smoothly.

All these tools are designed to get and keep your participants involved and connected to your session content. Chat windows, drawing tools, breakout rooms and polls are all parts of your webinar software platform you need to employ to make your webinar session a truly immersive experience.

Final thoughts about technology

Before you begin the work of designing your session, make sure your approach will work with the client, especially if you're using their in-house technology systems to connect with participants. Many organizations employ teams of technical professionals to install, maintain and update their business software, internet, intranet and related software and connections.

You need to be certain any company infrastructure won't get in the way of your delivery. For example, many organizations have adopted Voice over Internet Protocol (VoIP) telephony in their operations. This means they use the Internet for telephone connections. This may also mean that the participants won't have the option to "dial into" your session from their work telephone and will have to resort to using their personal phone or a cell phone.

Check in advance to make sure you won't run into trouble later.

Chapter 12: No time for the whole book?

Ten things to check off before you even f*cking start!

If you haven't time to read the whole book, or you're suddenly dumped into hosting or co-hosting a webinar with not much time to prepare, these ten items will help you make sure your session has the best possible chance of success. Addressing these key components will help ensure you've covered the basics.

Hopefully you'll be able to go back and read the rest of this book later, but for now this will help.

1 - Objective

- Who is your audience? What do <u>they</u> want to gain from your session?
- What are <u>your</u> intended outcomes from the session?
- What issues or problems are you addressing?
- What are attendees going to take away from your webinar?
- How soon will they be able to apply the new learning?

2 – Audio

- Have you heard yourself (recorded and played back)?
- What is your voice modulation like?
- Are you speaking clearly, slowly, and with enthusiasm for your subject?
- How stable is your webinar software when it comes to

the audio channel?

3 - Applicable

- How quickly can attendees apply the learning to their current problem?
- How relatable is your material for your intended audience?
- Does your content address your participants needs?

4 - Relevant

- How relevant are your examples? Do they reference actual work situations for your audience members or are they vague or too generalized?
- Does your material provide immediate tools or solutions for your participants?

5 – Memorable

- How 'sticky' is your material?
- What techniques are your using to make sure your lesson is cemented into long-term memory for your participants?

6 – Lean

- Have you trimmed out all the fat and fluff from your presentation?
- How wordy are your PowerPoint slides?
- Have you distilled your ideas down to the simplest and cleanest presentation possible?

7 – Engaging

- How quickly can you get participants engaged? What ice breaker exercises do you have planned?
- What webinar software tools are you employing? Polls? Chat? Whiteboard? Breakout room?
- Do you have an engagement opportunity built into your session at least every ten minutes?

8 – Genuine

- Are **you** looking forward to the session?
- Will your audience hear your enthusiasm and excitement? Are you contagious?
- Stay "in the moment" and don't lose focus.

9 – Facilitate

- Are you going to be the "guide on the side" or the "sage on the stage?" Facilitate; don't teach.
- Encourage participants to challenge, question and exchange ideas. Tap into the collective group knowledge and experience.
- Link your material to real-life experiences and connect those experiences to existing participant knowledge

10- Audience of One

- How personal and individual can you make the webinar experience for your participant?

- Are you using "singular" words and phrases rather than broader group sounding words? (i.e., "you", or "yours'" vs. "company" or 'team")
- Have you built in ways to encourage everyone in your webinar room to participate – even the wallflowers?

Checking these ten items will give you the best chance of success. Good luck!

Chapter 13: Professional tips for professionals

Suggestions for doctors, lawyers, teachers, and professional association members

Thousands of members of professional association have been forced online because of the pandemic. Now, not only do you have a professional reputation to maintain you need to maintain a professional online persona as well.

Whether you're a doctor seeing patients, a lawyer interviewing a client, a teacher working with a room full of students, or any other professional, there are a few "virtual" issues that directly impact you.

Chances are your regulatory authority has already sent out a set of guidelines or rules for conducting your business online. Check with your local authority to see what the acceptable standards are. If your association doesn't have such standards already in place, check to see if they are being developed or have been sent and you've missed them in the flurry of emails and exchanges that occurred over the past many months.

Recordings

Rather than making notes during the appointment and taking your eyes off the webcam (and your client) consider using the recording options available in your webinar software. This allows you to maintain a consistent focus on the person in front of you without being distracted by having to jot things down.

Use the technology suggestions from Chapter 11 to make sure your camera is adjusted so it doesn't look like you're looking down on your client. Don't sit too close to the webcam and make sure your audio is clean and clear. Depending on your profession, you may be discussing very personal and private details so maintain your attention and work to build trust with your client.

Privacy

The content of your discussion, as well as any recordings you choose to make, may set off a series of personal privacy concerns you'll need to address. Depending on your jurisdiction, there may be existing laws and regulations in the way you store and access personal information.

If you're recording sessions, you'll need to know where these recordings are stored, as well as what sort of encryption or protection there is in place against access by others. Who else might be able to access these recordings?

Minors

Teachers have an additional challenge in the virtual classroom as do many other professions when dealing with minors. It's difficult enough dealing with adults who aren't tech savvy, but meeting children online can be a major headache as well as an additional source of privacy concern.

Anyone working with minors in the virtual space must remember these additional steps.

First, ensure you can lock your virtual room. Programs like Zoom allow you to lock a session after you start so no one else can join. Give attendees a few minutes to "get in their seats" and then enable security settings to prevent others from dropping in.

Next, be aware of any screen sharing settings in your webinar software. If you have the option to adjust sharing privileges, make sure they're set to "Host only" so you're the only one able to share content with the group. You don't want someone to randomly share things they shouldn't or disrupt the session by sharing something off-topic.

Use your lobby or waiting room to protect your audience and keep out anyone who shouldn't be there. Using Zoom again as an example, you can set options for who ends up in the waiting room before the session starts. You could allow all participants to be sent to the virtual lobby where you can admit them to the session individually, or you can configure your set-up so participants sign in as "Guest Participants" which means only those who are invited to your session pop into the session and sends anyone else to the waiting room.

You can also control your session by locking down the chat window, thereby restricting crosstalk and preventing private messaging between attendees.

If someone does manage to get into the session despite your controls, you can always remove them from the session. Simply scroll over their name in your attendance list and click "Remove" from the drop-down options. They'll be kicked out of your session and won't be allowed back in.

Your professional association may have a set of guidelines or recommendations you can reference. Check with them to be sure your webinar sessions comply with your association's expectations and standards.

Lawyers: Some of the best practices for using video conferencing software when providing legal services or advice are summarized below:

- Confirm the client's consent to proceed in the virtual arena.
- Ask everyone to introduce themselves to everyone else in the virtual space.
- Ensure there is no one at the client's location who may improperly influence or interfere in the client's decisions.
- Be sure audio and video feeds are stable and you can hear and see all parties involved.
- If identification must be produced to support verification of identity, ensure a copy of the document (front and back) is sent to you in advance of the online meeting and that when the identification is produced the entire document is visible and legible.

- Determine how to provide clients copies of any documents executed remotely.
- Confirm your client's understanding about the documents they are executing and give adequate opportunity for them to ask questions during the video conference.
- Maintain detailed records including the date, start and end time, the method of communication, identity of all those present, and minutes of the meeting.

Again, check with your local authority to see what acceptable standards may already in place. There may be specific restrictions or recommendations that will apply.

Bonus Chapter 14: Tips and tricks for attendees

What to do when you're invited to a virtual meeting

Oh goody. Another F*cking Webinar!

You've just received the e-vite to the next Teams meeting with your cohorts- or the monthly Zoom meeting of your knitting club – or the virtual training session your employer has arranged. Are you excited?

Or are you dreading the mind-numbing two to three hours that lie ahead? Short of moving to a country without internet, how do you handle one more virtual meeting? Is there anything you can do to make the most of this new "normal" of connectivity?

It turns out, as a participant, you can do a **lot** of things to make the session as positive and productive as it can be – for yourself and everyone else involved.

Pre-work

Check your webinar invitation or login instructions for any links to pre-work for the session. Many webinar professionals will ask you to complete a few things prior to attending the session. If there are suggested videos to watch – carve out some time to watch them. You wouldn't be asked if this wasn't important, and they will set the stage for the best session outcomes. Webinar professionals today respect your time and they're not going to ask you to waste it on something that is unnecessary.

If you're asked to complete a form or provide some information, now is the time to do that. Again, if it wasn't important, you wouldn't be asked to do this. Complete any forms well in advance of the session start time. You don't want to be filling in any pertinent information or personal details you might need to look up at the last minute.

If the invitation contains links to test the webinar room connections, or audio set-up, then set aside some time to do that before logging into the live event. Not only will you be making sure YOU can connect and hear things, but you also won't be taking time from the session trying to test things after the scheduled start time of the session. None of us like to sit idly by while someone fiddles around with their audio connections delaying the start of the webinar (and you don't want to be that someone).

Show up on time

If your session gives a start time, be respectful and show up at least five minutes in advance. This can prove to be a useful networking opportunity.

Think of those pre-Covid events you attended when someone burst through the training room doors two minutes after everyone had settled in and introduced themselves. What did you think of that person? Do you want folks to put you into that same category?

Showing up in advance does two things – both to your advantage. First, it allows you to make sure your connections to the session are working. If you have audio or video issues, it's always easier to correct them ahead of the session than during the event when you're disrupting the experience for everyone else.

Second, it gives you the opportunity to connect with the presenter and everyone else in the session. This is vital to the overall success of the session and, more importantly, to what you will take away from the event.

Knowing who is in the room, learning a little about the people you're sharing this experience with, sharing a few details – all this allows us to create a virtual space that closely resembles the physical space. If you were attending this session in a meeting room in the physical world, you'd be chatting around the coffee urn – sharing stories – catching up with co-workers – so try to make this webinar experience the same.

Get involved

When the facilitator asks for input – get up there! You don't need to dominate the space, but don't sit back and let the session proceed without your input.

You may not be inclined to speak up in the physical training room (hello Introverts), but you certainly have a level playing field in the virtual space. Even if your natural tendency is to sit on the sidelines and let others answer questions, you need to type into that chat window or text onto that whiteboard like you own it! Not only will you be contributing to the overall content and quality of the session, but you'll be also flexing some virtual muscle you can use in subsequent virtual events (and as I've said before – this virtual stuff is not going away).

Stay connected

Avoid checking your email just because you get a ping or notification. Don't be distracted from what is happening on the screen in front of you. The moment you take your eyes off the meeting, you'll start to find other things to focus on, and that's a sure-fire way to disconnect and lose the thread of the session.

If you attend multiple online events like I do, get in the habit of putting your phone on DND or even turning it off for the allotted time. Unless you're a heart surgeon and lives are at risk, chances are none of us are doing work that will result in someone dying if we don't respond to their email or text in the next hour or two. Focus on what is in front of you rather than being distracted by bings, chirps, ringtones, and pop-ups. Remember, you're doing this for you – to get maximum value out of the event and not simply sit through another f*cking webinar.

Speak up

Virtual spaces are often seen as a lot safer than physical spaces for people to speak up and contribute. Unlike meeting rooms where supervisors or senior executives might be on the periphery "observing" and unintentionally intimidating people from speaking their mind, the virtual space allows people the opportunity to contribute without feeling like they're being judged. (Ideally, your webinar host will have set up these ground rules in advance with the webinar sponsor.)

If you're asked a question – provide an answer. Even if it's off the mark, you'll be seen as adding content that can be discussed and you wind up being a part of the experience. Don't hog the stage, but don't be a wallflower either.

Connect peer-to-peer

During the session, you may find kindred spirits you share ideals with. Make a point of maintaining and continuing those connections. Some of the best learning that comes from virtual sessions doesn't happen in the session itself, but rather after the event when participants connect one-to-one to share stories, ideas, and solutions.

I've hosted sessions that have introduced people to others who have become lifelong friends, confidants, and collaborators. Learning how others are applying the learning in their situations can often help us see ways to adapt it to fit our roles. Peer-to-peer connections can be a vital part of our career growth.

Provide feedback

Professional presenters need to know how the session landed. They're constantly recalibrating and tweaking their material to make sure it's connecting correctly with participants. If you're given the opportunity to fill in a post-session survey or follow up questionnaire – do it. Your perception of the event is vital to ensuring future participants receive the best possible experience. Professional presenters can take negative feedback so don't worry about hurting their feelings. Honest constructive feedback allows them to adjust and improve their future sessions.

If the presenter doesn't refer you to a post-session feedback form, ask about one. Sometimes in the final few minutes, presenters are speeding through those last few slides and wrapping things up before closing out the session, so it may just slip their mind. By asking for a link to the feedback form, you may be helping them remember an important item they've overlooked.

If the session doesn't have a feedback form, connect with the presenter directly after the session and offer any thoughts or comments you have. I've had attendees reach out to me after a webinar to clarify something they didn't quite understand during the session, and I was happy to answer their questions and revisit the material.

That next webinar doesn't have to be a time suck or mind-numbing experience and you have the power to help make future sessions better by following these few suggestions.

As a webinar participant, you can really help shape the virtual experience for others in the future.

Chapter 15: In conclusion

You have an obligation to every one of your attendees to deliver a professional experience. Remember to invest an **"ARM and a LEG"** into every session.

Get in the habit of using good attendance sheets. They're a great way to keep connected to the individuals in your session and a lifesaver in some situations.

Pay attention to your voice, the words you choose, horse feathers, and remember to smile and have fun. If you're enjoying the session there's a good chance your attendees are enjoying it too. Be contagions!

Use all the tools you're comfortable with to keep participants involved. Beginning in the lobby or waiting room and rolling right through to the last slide, remember that this session is for them – not you. Always keep the attendee at the centre of your focus – and remember that "audience of one".

Power up those PowerPoint slides! I can't over emphasize this. Don't read what you've put into text. Use images and graphics as much as possible. Use transitions and animations wisely. Avoid the "font of the week" syndrome and keep slides simple, bright, and uncluttered.

Watch your use of humour – not everyone finds the same thing funny, and some jokes can fall flat and ruin your status as a webinar professional.

If you're translating your classroom presentation to the

virtual space, remember the very different experiences afforded in virtual and adjust your slide deck accordingly. Don't leave slides up on the screen for extended periods of time while you natter on in the background. Use bullet points to bring in concepts or ideas one by one.

Get buy-in and collaboration early, beginning in the lobby or waiting room. Use ice breakers to get folks familiar with others in the session. Encourage idea sharing and cross-pollination of ideas.

Build in some sort of participant interaction at least every ten minutes. It could be a poll, a whiteboard exercise, a quiz, or a discussion via the chat window – your choice. Keep them participating to keep them engaged.

Remember to constantly check the pulse of the session. Pause for questions. Ask for input or feedback. If you must, call on folks who haven't contributed for a while to make sure they're paying attention and still engaged. Don't put them on the spot but rather encourage them to add to the on-going discussion. "Lori – we haven't heard your thoughts on this yet. Would you like to add anything to what's been discussed?"

Facilitate, don't lecture. The accumulated experience of everyone in your webinar room is an asset – be sure to tap into that and encourage the sharing of ideas and thoughts. I've often seen some off-the-cuff comment from a participant suddenly become a light bulb moment for someone else in the session. And you can't buy that kind of memorability when it comes to getting value out of a webinar.

Keep the "ARM & a LEG" principals in mind. Make sure your presentation is:

Applicable – what can they take away today and use immediately?

Keep your presentation **Relevant** to the needs of the group by using examples that meet their needs.

How **Memorable** can you make this event? How special or sticky was this learning experience? What will participants remember two weeks from now? Six months from now? How do you anchor this experience in long-term memory?

Keep it **Lean** – strip your slide deck and verbiage down to the bare basics. Whenever possible, use images instead of text and don't read slides verbatim.

Engage your attendees; keep them contributing and collaborating on their own journey.

And be **Genuine;** you may have delivered the session a dozen times – or a hundred - but it's the first time for your audience, so it must sound fresh and new.

Does your choice of technology help or hinder the learner? Don't pick a particular software because it's easier for YOU to use. While that **is** an important consideration, what is more important is how easy it is for your **USER** to use. Any platform you choose must first be user friendly from the participant's point of view. If they find the webinar software difficult, they'll find your session taxing.

Keep these points in mind when designing your next webinar. You'll be seen as a real webinar professional.

Best wishes, and happy virtual facilitating!

Dale Nelson, Vancouver, Canada

Resources:

PowerPoint training sessions

Microsoft PowerPoint training from Microsoft: available here https://support.microsoft.com/en-us/office/powerpoint-for-windows-training-40e8c930-cb0b-40d8-82c4-bd53d3398787

There are also free and paid online PowerPoint tutorials and training sessions from companies such as SkillShare. You can check them out here: https://www.skillshare.com

Adobe Connect

Adobe is a company most of us have heard about. They've been pioneers in graphics software and PDF handling for years. Adobe Connect has been around for years and is still a powerful webinar software program.

Key features include:

- It provides a variety of templates to customize your virtual environments.
- It helps you create unique registration pages.
- Ability to influence and reach out to target audience with videos, blogs, surveys, and polls.
- It offers robust analytics for better insights.
- Integrates easily with CRM software like Eloqua and Salesforce.

PRICING PACKAGES: (as listed November 2021)

Adobe Connect comes with a moderate price tag. For 100

seats, it is $130.00 per month, $470.00 per month for 500 seats, and $580.00 per month for 1,000 seats. Each plan allows you to host unlimited events. Moreover, you get a 30-day free trial to test out the product.

CONS:

There have been some rare instances of display video and audio compatibility issues in mobile devices.

One of the highest prices for webinar software.

Cisco WebEx

For security reasons alone, you can't beat WebEx, and with a company like Cisco behind it, that stands to reason. WebEx provides some impressive features like HD video and audio services that are accessible on multiple devices. There's a fair amount of customization available for the host so you can tweak the webinar room to suit the audience.

Through WebEx webinars, you can hold meetings throughout your organization, offer online and offline training sessions, and provide remote support. The key USPs of WebEx include mobility, user-friendliness, and compatibility with all devices and browsers.

KEY FEATURES:

- Cloud-based platform so along with superior speed, you gain data security too.
- It allows you to host up to 40,000 attendees.
- Built-in Q&A sessions, polls, and surveys to facilitate

audience engagement.

- It provides a mobile app.
- Strong customer service.
- The excellent HD video and audio quality.
- Integrates with popular marketing tools like Salesforce.

PRICING PACKAGES: (as listed November 2021)

The Basic plan costs $13.50 per month for up to 50 participants if billed annually. The price climbs up as you move on to a higher-tier plan.

CONS:

More suited for in-house team collaboration than webinars.

Google Hangouts

One of the most popular names on this list, Google Hangouts is a completely free solution that easily integrates with the Chrome Browser and Gmail. You can either host a webinar for up to 30 prospects or stream it on YouTube to invite a larger audience base.

Google Hangouts is one of the best free software choices because it caters to every business size, whether a small or medium-sized business or a large corporation. It also allows several people to speak and share their screen during the webinar and record the meetings.

Since it's free, there are some main downsides compared to other tools listed. For example, while it's good for quick 1-to-

1 meetings you don't get any automation or marketing features.

KEY FEATURES:

- Allows up to 30 people in the chat.
- Several speakers can speak during the webinar.
- Completely free of cost.
- The recording is done automatically and uploaded on your YouTube channel right away.
- It can create a webinar in 10 seconds.
- Integrates with YouTube and Chrome.
- No additional software download needed.
- Easy screenshare features.

PRICING PACKAGES: (as listed November 2021)

Free, but limited for those looking to optimize their sales funnel.

CONS:

A Google account is a prerequisite.

Google Hangouts does not offer any other additional marketing features, such as analytics, paid events, email marketing, etc.

Zoom

Zoom is one of the most popular webinar software programs on the market today, connecting friends and colleagues worldwide across different time zones.

Some reasons to use Zoom is that it's intuitive, entirely cloud-based, and has a user-friendly interface that makes things easy for its users.

It performs a wide array of activities that make it an asset to any company. Zoom offers HD video and audio, screen sharing, desktop, and app sharing options.

Additionally, it allows you to host the scheduled and unscheduled meeting and keeps a backup of every session in the cloud for ready and instant access later.

Their web conferencing software also allows private and public chats so that the audience does not necessarily have to interrupt the speaker while he or she is making a point.

It also integrates with Google Calendar and Microsoft Outlook, which allows its users to schedule meetings and send emails seamlessly. Zoom is a one-stop-shop for everything when it comes to hosting a webinar event.

KEY FEATURES:

- HD video and audio, along with screens sharing facility.
- Desktop and app sharing options.
- Backup of every meeting in the cloud.
- It allows private and public chats, which lets your viewers communicate during the event without any interruption.
- Provides free access to up to 100 participants and 40 mins limit on group meetings.

- Efficient host controls and virtual whiteboards.
- User-friendly and easily navigable dashboard.
- There are no one-time fees and it's free to sign up.

PRICING PACKAGES: (as listed November 2021)

It is one of the best webinar platforms that provide a freemium package. The free plan offers 40 minutes on the webinar and allows up to 100 participants. The Basic paid plan offers every feature along with 1 GB of cloud recording and costs $14.99 per host per month.

The Business package, ideal for small and medium-sized businesses, is $19.99 per host per month and can accommodate up to 300 participants. The Enterprise package, which is best suited for large enterprises, costs $19.99 per host per month and can accommodate up to 1000 participants.

CONS:

- Some reviews suggest that the audio quality should be improved.
- Some users have complained that the calls get automatically disconnected sometimes.
- Zoom is great for quick meetings, but it doesn't have the deep marketing and automation features some others have.

Image Bank links

Shutterstock https://www.shutterstock.com

Adobe stock images https://www.stock.adobe.com/images

Depositphotos: https://www.depositphotos.com/

Megapixl.com: https://www.megapixl.com

Unsplash: https://unsplash.com

Getty Images: https://www.gettyimages.com

Image Editing links

GIMP - https://www.gimp.org/

Adobe Photoshop Lightroom
https://www.adobe.com/ca/products/photoshop-lightroom.html

Microsoft Photos app included with Windows 10-
accessible by clicking the Windows icon and selecting Photos
from your application directory

Flickr - https://www.flickr.com/

Google Photos - https://www.google.com/photos/about/

Photofx - https://photofx.net/

LinkedIn Learning

LinkedIn Learning is another resource for learning
PowerPoint tips and tricks. You can get a free month trial of
LinkedIn Learning. Visit their site here:
https://www.linkedin.com/learning

For a deeper dive into personality types, check out tools like Myers Briggs Type Indicator (MBTI) https://www.myersbriggs.org/my-mbti-personality-type/mbti-basics/

or Insights Learning and Development https://www.insights.com/

Glossary of terms

Chat (or chat bar): an interactive component of most webinar software programs allowing participants to communicate in text with the presenter or other participants. Like text messaging in real time.

e-Learning: any type of training or information session conducted using a computer or electronic device connected to the internet and accessing a webinar software program.

Emoji: a pictogram, logogram, ideogram, or smiley used in electronic messages and web pages. The primary function of emojis is to fill in emotional cues otherwise missing from typed conversation. Some examples of emojis are ,

F2F: Face-to-face, an in-person meeting with meeting participants in the same physical space. A live interaction in real time.

Interactive tools: features contained in most webinar software programs designed to allow participants and presenters to engage with each other. Examples include polls, chat windows, whiteboards, breakout rooms.

Poll (or polling): an interactive tool within most webinar programs allowing the presenter to create short polls including Q&A questions. Designed to gain feedback from course content and enhance audience engagement.

Status (or status icon): a notification feature built into most webinar programs that allows participants to notify the presenter if they wish to speak (i.e., raise a hand) or ask the presenter to speak louder, slow down, or to toggle emojis to express applause, laughter, etc.

USP: unique selling point; the one feature or perceived benefit of a good or service that makes it unique from the rest of the competing brands in the market. Every product should have its own USP to make it stand apart from other products in the similar category.

VoIP: Voice over Internet Protocol, also called IP telephony, is a method and group of technologies for the delivery of voice communications and multimedia sessions over Internet Protocol networks, such as the Internet.

Webinar: a seminar conducted over the internet

Whiteboard: an interactive tool included with many webinars software programs which allows multiple participants and presenters to 'write' or participate on the screen just like there were writing on a flip chart or physical whiteboard.

About the author

An award-winning newspaper publisher and writer for radio and television, Dale spent many years in marketing and communications. He began instructing in the webinar space over a decade ago. Long before Covid-19 restrictions forced organizations to pivot to the virtual space, Dale was crafting and delivering virtual learning  experiences to clients around the world. Beginning in 2015 he delivered monthly on-line webinars to people from all walks of life. He has used a variety of webinar software platforms and has become familiar with some of their quirks as well as some of their advantages.

He has kept a notebook of almost every mistake that can be made in the virtual space, and nearly everything that can go wrong. The list of Pro Tips he shares in this book as well as his *"ARM and a LEG"* principles were developed to make sure when you are developing virtual sessions, they deliver maximum value to everyone – participants, sponsors, and you, the presenter.

Dale lives in Vancouver, Canada. Contact the author at dale@professionalwebinars.com or visit his website https://www.professionalwebinars.com.